# JOIN THE TRIUMPH OF THE SKIES!

# JOIN THE TRIUMPH OF THE SKIES!

## 31 Reasons to Celebrate Christmas

**DAVE MALLINAK**

XULON PRESS

Xulon Press
2301 Lucien Way #415
Maitland, FL 32751
407.339.4217
www.xulonpress.com

**xulon**
PRESS

Paperback ISBN-13: 978-1-66286-293-9
Ebook ISBN-13: 978-1-66286-294-6

For my wife Belinda.
You are the crown to my head and the jewel in the crown.
Thank you for your steadfast love over these many years, for
being the wife I needed and the mother our children wanted.
Thank you for the idea.

And for Berean Baptist Church.
You have proved yourselves to be true Bereans and have
blessed our family more than you will ever know.
This book is for you. I hope you find it delightful and that it
adds to your Christmas celebrations.

Hark! The herald angels sing,
"Glory to the newborn King;
Peace on earth, and mercy mild,
God and sinners reconciled!"
Joyful, all ye nations rise,
Join the triumph of the skies;
With th'angelic host proclaim,
"Christ is born in Bethlehem!"

Hark! the herald angels sing,
"Glory to the newborn King!"

Christ, by highest Heav'n adored;
Christ the everlasting Lord;
Late in time, behold Him come,
Offspring of a virgin's womb.
Veiled in flesh the Godhead see;
Hail th'incarnate Deity,
Pleased with us in flesh to dwell,
Jesus our Emmanuel.

Hark! the herald angels sing,
"Glory to the newborn King!"

Hail the heav'nly Prince of Peace!
Hail the Sun of Righteousness!
Light and life to all He brings,
Ris'n with healing in His wings.
Mild He lays His glory by,
Born that man no more may die;
Born to raise the sons of earth,

Born to give them second birth.

Hark! the herald angels sing,
"Glory to the newborn King!"

Come, Desire of nations, come,
Fix in us Thy humble home;
Rise, the woman's conqu'ring Seed,
Bruise in us the serpent's head.
Now display Thy saving pow'r,
Ruined nature now restore;
Now in mystic union join
Thine to ours, and ours to Thine.

Hark! the herald angels sing,
"Glory to the newborn King!"

Adam's likeness, Lord, efface,
Stamp Thine image in its place:
Second Adam from above,
Reinstate us in Thy love.
Let us Thee, though lost, regain,
Thee, the Life, the inner man:
Oh, to all Thyself impart,
Formed in each believing heart.

Hark! the herald angels sing,
"Glory to the newborn King!"

Original lyrics by Charles Wesley

# Table of Contents

# A Note to the Reader

D ear Friend,

Please consider this little collection of Christmas meditations a gift from our family to yours. Our only desire with this book is to share a little of the joy and delight we find each year at Christmas.

Christmas in the Mallinak Family begins on schedule right after Thanksgiving and stretches into early January. Before our children were born, God moved my wife and me 1,400 miles away from our nearest family for ministry in Utah. As God began to give us children, we decided to stay home for Christmas and develop our own Christmas traditions built around the Word of God and a special delight in God's unspeakable gift to the world. Family traditions included decorating the Christmas tree (always a family affair), advent calendars, special meals, squirreling presents until Christmas Eve, movies (none of them Hallmark), and a family gathering each evening to read from a Christmas devotional.

I don't remember our family ever suffering from the Christmas blues on December 26. The credit for this probably goes to my wife, who dreamed up a great tradition that spanned Christmas Day and stretched into January. Each non-holiday during Christmas, she would have a unique theme for the day.

One day the kids would be knights; another day, cowboys; another day would be pioneer day; another would be pirate day. As soon as she announced what day it was, the kids would scurry off to dress for the occasion. On pioneer day, she would set up our dining room chairs like a wagon, throw a sheet over the top, and the kids would drive the wagon across the prairie. On one particular pirate day, one of the kids ran to their room, grabbed a black magic marker, and colored a full beard and mustache on their face before we could stop it. We had church that night, and the marker didn't exactly wash away in time, so that child got to go to church with a greenish beard.

As the kids grew older, we noticed how much these family traditions meant to them. They would beg their mom to do those special days even when the oldest kids advanced deep into their teen years. When our daughter went to college, she would start into the Christmas music late in August, even before Labor Day. But I think the best assurance that our family celebrations profoundly impacted their lives came when our oldest son started working a job to save for college. Around the end of November, as he came home from work one day, he said, "Dad, I can't believe how many people hate Christmas!" He had been expressing his excitement for the start of the holiday season and was shocked to learn that most people are regular Scrooges. He couldn't understand that.

From the time the kids were little, we made Christmas about the coming of Christ. The most important way we did this was by reading from a Christmas devotional each night. The first devotional we found was Douglas Wilson's *God Rest Ye Merry*, and for many years, we read that book from cover to cover during December. My debts to that book will be evident in this little book. I made a valiant effort to give credit to any ideas that came directly from it, but it is impossible to cite every place in this book that was inspired by something he said. So, I will simply say to him, "Thank you. You blessed our family with your own delight in the Christmas story."

After several years of reading Wilson's book, we found Joel Beeke's book *When Christ Came: 31 Meditations on the Incarnation.* That book blessed our family tremendously, and I used it to develop a Christmas sermon series, some of which ended up in this book. And most recently, we picked up a fine book called *The Christmas We Didn't Expect* by David Mathis. Again, our family was richly blessed by the author's thoughts on the first coming of Christ.

Last Christmas, we decided to give a devotional book to our fellow members at church in hopes that we could encourage them to do what we do each December. As we were mulling over the choices, my wife commented: "you should write one yourself."

So, I did. I wrote this book for Berean Baptist Church, where I have had the joy of pastoring for many more years than I have deserved. God richly blessed our family by uniting us to such a wonderful fellowship of believers. This book is my gift to you, a way of saying "thank you" for your love and friendship and faithfulness through the years. You stood by me when I wasn't easy to stand by, supported me when I needed your support, encouraged me to grow in the Lord and my ability to be your pastor, and blessed my family and me in countless ways. God bless you all, and Merry Christmas to you!

If my little contribution to your Christmas celebration blesses you and your family and deepens your love for Christ, it will have accomplished its purpose. I trust that the joy of the Lord will be your strength, that the peace that passes understanding will keep your heart and mind this Christmas, and that God will bless you in December and throughout the years.

# Reason #1: Because It Was a Long Time Coming

> But when the fulness of the time was come, God sent forth his Son, made of a woman, made under the law, To redeem them that were under the law, that we might receive the adoption of sons. (Galatians 4:4-5)

**P**erhaps no phrase torments quite like the phrase "not yet." Among the ways we torture our children, it ranks just a little above "we'll see" and "you'll have to wait." "Dad, are we there yet?" "Not yet." "When will it be Christmas?" "Not yet." "Can we open our presents now?" "Not yet." "Are we finished cleaning our bedrooms?" "Not yet." "Can I be finished eating my spinach?" "Not yet." As a child, my parents banned certain words from my vocabulary. I wanted to give them a banned list, too – and "not yet" was near the top of that list.

For thousands of years, the people of God wondered when the Messiah would come. The prophets enquired. The devout Israelites longed and desired. But for thousands of years, God said, "Not yet." During the 1,000 years of Adam's life, God said, "Not yet." During the generations of Noah, God said, "Not yet." In the days of Abraham and Isaac and Jacob, God said, "Not yet." During the 400 years while Israel sojourned in the land of Egypt, God said, "Not yet." When the Pharaoh came who knew not Joseph, while Israel toiled under their Egyptian taskmasters, God said, "Not yet." During the 40 years that Israel wandered in the wilderness, God said, "Not yet." In the time of Israel's rebellion, when their kings turned them against God and the prophets cried out for repentance and revival, God said, "Not yet." When the Assyrians conquered the Northern ten tribes, God said, "Not yet." When the Babylonians carried Judah into captivity, God said, "Not yet." In the nearly 400 years after Malachi, before the birth of Jesus Christ, God said, "Not yet."

Not until we had time to prove that our wisdom was folly and our strength weakness. Not until we showed ourselves unfaithful, our religious efforts empty and vain. Not until we demonstrated that 1,500 years of Old Covenant offerings and sacrifices and ordinances could not reform us. Not until we established our hopelessly fallen condition did God say, "Now."

The Bible says, "when the fullness of the time was come." I don't know what triggered this "fullness of the time." God alone knows His heart and thoughts; they are higher than I can think. But when God sent His Son, this much I do know: it was the right time. It was the time God chose.

As we "join the triumph of the skies" this Christmas, I invite you to rejoice in God's timing. Jesus was born at the right time, at the perfect time in history. He entered our world at the time God chose. Three things should stir our hearts to celebrate.

First, *God sent forth His Son.* God entered our world. He inserted Himself into our situation. The Son He sent was "made of a woman, made under the law." That is, He was fully human. He was not a special kind of human or a new kind of humanity. God did not create a different type of human nature than what we are. God made Himself in every way what we are – in every way human. All of humanity is under the law, so He joined us under the law. Jesus did not make Himself above the law. He did not make Himself the law, though He was the Law-maker and the Law-giver. He demonstrated that He was made under the law by being circumcised according to the law on the 8th day. Throughout His life, He went about doing good. He did no evil; neither was any guile found in His mouth.

> Think not that I am come to destroy the law, or the prophets: I am not come to destroy, but to fulfil. (Matthew 5:17)

Second, God sent forth His Son *to redeem them that were under the law*. "Redeem" means "to buy out of the slave market."[1] Not the slave market of sin, but the slave market *of the law*. Jesus redeemed us from the *bondage* of the law; we are no longer bound by all those prohibitions and washings and offerings. He redeemed us from the *condemnation* of the law. The law exposes our sin and condemns us for sinning. The law tells us what to do but gives us no strength to do it. Christ redeemed us from the curse of the law by being made a curse for us. (Galatians 3:13)

Thirdly, God sent forth His Son *that we might receive the adoption of sons*. Redemption re-positions us as sons of God rather than our former position as slaves under the bondage of the law. Jesus changes our status before God. He makes us heirs. He gives us an inheritance. He grants us a right to what is His. The servant needs permission to use the household goods. A son has a right to it. God's Son became a man so He could make men into sons. God sent His Son because He wanted more sons. And this is God's triumph: *the triumph of the skies!*

# Reason #2: Because the Prophets Said He Would Come

> Yea, and all the prophets from Samuel and those that follow after, as many as have spoken, have likewise foretold of these days. (Acts 3:24)

G od keeps His promises. And the promise of the Messiah underlies every other promise God made. God had the Messiah in mind when He promised Adam and Eve:

> And I will put enmity between thee and the woman, and between thy seed and her seed; it shall bruise thy head, and thou shalt bruise his heel. (Genesis 3:15)

The promise of the Messiah was back of God's promise to Abraham:

> And I will make of thee a great nation, and I will bless thee, and make thy name great; and thou shalt be a blessing: And I will bless them that bless thee, and curse him that curseth thee: and in thee shall all families of the earth be blessed. (Genesis 12:2-3)

When God promised to establish the throne of David's seed forever, He meant the Messiah.

> And when thy days be fulfilled, and thou shalt
> sleep with thy fathers, I will set up thy seed after
> thee, which shall proceed out of thy bowels, and
> I will establish his kingdom. He shall build an
> house for my name, and I will stablish the throne
> of his kingdom for ever. (2 Samuel 7:12-13)

The promise of the Messiah fills the Old Testament. Every prophet, every priest, and every king points to Christ. The entire sacrificial system foretells Him. Moses' Tabernacle and Solomon's Temple anticipate His coming. Every Old Testament story references the coming Messiah.

> Comfort ye, comfort ye my people, saith your
> God. Speak ye comfortably to Jerusalem, and
> cry unto her, that her warfare is accomplished,
> that her iniquity is pardoned: for she hath
> received of the LORD'S hand double for all
> her sins. The voice of him that crieth in the
> wilderness, Prepare ye the way of the LORD,
> make straight in the desert a highway for our
> God. Every valley shall be exalted, and every
> mountain and hill shall be made low: and the
> crooked shall be made straight, and the rough
> places plain: And the glory of the LORD shall
> be revealed, and all flesh shall see it together:
> for the mouth of the LORD hath spoken it.
> (Isaiah 40:1-5)

George Frederic Handel dedicated the entire first part of his *Messiah* to Old Testament prophecy concerning Jesus. The words, which are taken almost verbatim from the King James Version of Scripture, set forth as fine a summary of the prophetic promise as you will find.

> Behold, I will send my messenger, and he shall prepare the way before me: and the Lord, whom ye seek, shall suddenly come to his temple, even the messenger of the covenant, whom ye delight in: behold, he shall come, saith the LORD of hosts. But who may abide the day of his coming? and who shall stand when he appeareth? for he is like a refiner's fire, and like fullers' soap: And he shall sit as a refiner and purifier of silver: and he shall purify the sons of Levi, and purge them as gold and silver, that they may offer unto the LORD an offering in righteousness. (Malachi 3:1-3)

Think of the triumph in God's promise. Time after time, it seemed that the godly line of Seth had come to its end. Judah's sons died without an heir, yet, through a scandalous sin, God raised up an heir to Judah. God raised up another son through the harlot Rahab. Boaz was an old bachelor when God brought Ruth to give him a son. God raised up Solomon through David and Bathsheba.

> Blessed be the LORD, that hath given rest unto his people Israel, according to all that he promised: there hath not failed one word of all his good promise, which he promised by the hand of Moses his servant. (I Kings 8:56)

The kingly line survived slavery in Egypt, the years of wandering in the wilderness, the giant Goliath, the ruthless pursuit of King Saul, captivity in Babylon, and the nearly 400 years while God was silent. Only after all this did that night of nights come when Jesus was born.

The forces of hell made many attempts to prevent the Messiah from completing His mission. Those efforts only intensified after His birth. Herod ordered the slaughter of every child in Bethlehem and in all the coasts thereof, from two years old and under. The people of Nazareth tried to throw him off the brow of the hill where their city was built. The Jews took up stones to stone Him. But they could not stop Him.

And on the cross, they couldn't kill Him either. They tried. They beat Him, mocked Him, scourged Him, crowned Him with a crown of thorns, laid His cross on Him, laid Him on His cross, nailed Him to it, and did everything in their power to kill Him. They used the cruelest tortures ever invented by man to end His life. But He survived it all. And when He had drained the cup of the wrath of God to the very dregs, He Who laid down His life willingly for His people cried out, "It is finished," and He gave up the ghost.

> Therefore doth my Father love me, because I lay down my life, that I might take it again. No man taketh it from me, but I lay it down of myself. I have power to lay it down, and I have power to take it again. (John 10:17-18)

The same prophets who prophesied the birth of Christ also prophesied that He would die. But the prophecy didn't end there. They promised that Jesus would rise from the dead, that corruption would not take Him, and that death would not keep Him. It did not. Jesus rose from the dead, triumphant over death itself. Because He lives, we shall live also. And the care God has taken to fulfill all of His good word assures us that Jesus is coming again.

> For ye have need of patience, that, after ye have done the will of God, ye might receive the promise. For yet a little while, and he that shall come will come, and will not tarry. (Hebrews 10:36-37)

Join the triumph of the skies!

# Reason #3: Because Celebrations are So Christian

Let the heavens rejoice, and let the earth be glad; let the sea roar, and the fulness thereof. Let the field be joyful, and all that is therein: then shall all the trees of the wood rejoice Before the LORD: for he cometh, for he cometh to judge the earth: he shall judge the world with righteousness, and the people with his truth. (Psalm 96:11-13)

H.L. Menken defined Puritanism as "the haunting fear that someone, somewhere, may be happy."[2] Whether or not the Puritans rejected happiness is a discussion for another day. But unfortunately, more than a few Christians identify with the cranky types.

Nothing brings out the curmudgeons quite like Christmas, what with all its commercialism and Christmas trees and caroling and consumerism. So, as we launch into December, I thought we should prod the curmudgeons with a bit of Christmas cheer. I consider Christmas "the most wonderful time of the year," and I think it a worthy pursuit to promote a little joy, a little delight, and a whole lot of buildup for this celebration.

Should we celebrate Christmas? The Cranks tell us that December 25th was a pagan holiday. "Christians are celebrating the winter solstice!" "The Christmas tree is an idol!"

"God forbids our putting a tree in our house" (Jeremiah 10:1-6). Besides, where do you find jingling bells and silly hats in the Bible?

It can be tough to maintain the standard fume and sulk in December, but some will push through the holiday cheer and keep a sour face. Yet I have to think that unbelievers might wonder at a Christian who won't celebrate Christmas. The world considers it a Christian holiday. That's why they hate it. They don't want to hear "Merry Christmas." Their bah-hum-bugging has nothing to do with winter solstice or idolatrous trees in living rooms. The world knows what Christmas means. The former Soviet Union didn't ban Christmas trees because they were pagan.

Maybe some should re-think their opposition to Christmas celebrations. After all, what offers a more worthy occasion for a good birthday party than the birth of Christ? No, I don't know His birth date, and yes, I admit that December 25th could be arbitrary – maybe even established by less-than-godly men. Still, our Lord entered our world to save us. We should celebrate that.

The birth of Jesus Christ is the launch point of God's plan for our salvation. Everything starts there. Without the Incarnation, there would be no salvation. That is worth celebrating.

If the curmudgeons start digging in their heels, let me point out that celebration is a distinctly Christian activity. The Bible not only allows for such things but actually requires them. The Bible staggers us with its calendar full of celebrations and feasts.

- Abraham made a great feast the same day Isaac was weaned (Genesis 21:8).

- God demanded that Pharaoh let His people go "that they may hold a feast unto me in the wilderness" (Exodus 5:1).

- When God delivered Israel in the time of Esther, they created their own feast to remember that event (Esther 9:19).

- All the days of the afflicted are evil: but he that is of a merry heart hath a continual feast (Proverbs 15:15).

- God ordained the Sabbath as a weekly feast day (Leviticus 23:1-3).

- God established three official feasts (Exodus 23:14-17; Deuteronomy 16:16), and throughout the Bible, life revolved around those feasts. Even our Lord Jesus Christ organized His life around those feasts.

- Nor did Jesus limit Himself to the God-ordained feasts. From all indications, He celebrated Purim in John 5, a feast that harkened back to the book of Esther. He did the same with Hanukkah, the Feast of Dedication (John 10:22).

Is Biblical Christianity suspicious of joy or happiness? I think not. The Bible mentions happiness and joy so often that it stands as the preeminent authority on these things. No other source speaks more decisively on the subject.

So, it is good to celebrate. Joy is fruit of the Spirit. God blesses us with happiness and laughter. And if any holiday gives us cause for good cheer, it is Christmas. Think of what we celebrate on this day! Our Creator God made Himself one of us – what He had created. He entered our world to redeem us and deliver us from our sin. He saves us so that we can be blessed forever. What Christian wouldn't celebrate such a thing?!

I say, let The Cranks complain. I'm listening to my Christmas music right now and don't have time for debate. I'm setting up a tree in my living room. I do the lights. My wife and kids do the decorations. I hope you'll do the same. Get yourself a gaudy tree: the more lights, the better. While you're at it, drink some eggnog, buy some great gifts, break out the chocolate, wish for snow, and make sure your neighbors all know that you are a Christian. Because you celebrate Christmas. Join the triumph of the skies!

# Reason #4: Because Of His Unspeakable Glory

> The heavens declare the glory of God; and the firmament sheweth his handywork. Day unto day uttereth speech, and night unto night sheweth knowledge. There is no speech nor language, where their voice is not heard. (Psalm 19:1-3)

E verything in the created world speaks of the Creator God, who spoke into existence all that is. "The worlds were framed by the word of God." Our world and the created universe are spoken words – some have referred to it as a "spoken world." And that world shouts the glory of our Creator.

But nothing expresses the Creator's glory quite so eloquently or exhaustively as the Lord Jesus Christ. Jesus is the very glory of God – the brightness of His glory and the express image of His person (Hebrews 1:3). The shepherds and wise men, Mary and Joseph, and whoever else visited the manger in Bethlehem beheld in a tiny infant the very glory of God.

> And the Word was made flesh, and dwelt among us, (and we beheld his glory, the glory as of the only begotten of the Father,) full of grace and truth. (John 1:14)

Those who denied His glory, who refused to see it and fought against it, were squeezing their eyes shut against the

13

majesty of God Himself in human flesh. For Jesus is Immanuel, "God with us." Satan, as one of his evil works in our world, blinds men to the glory of God in the Person of Christ.

> In whom the god of this world hath blinded the minds of them which believe not, lest the light of the glorious gospel of Christ, who is the image of God, should shine unto them. (2 Corinthians 4:4)

Yet, we still see His glory in our world today – as clearly now as ever. For nature itself displays that glory in such a way as to leave men inexcusable.

> For the invisible things of him from the creation of the world are clearly seen, being understood by the things that are made, even his eternal power and Godhead; so that they are without excuse: (Romans 1:20)

The written Word of God in the 66 books of the Old and New Testaments sets forth the glory of Jesus Christ. When we read the Bible, we can't help but see His glory painted in brilliant detail. The portrait of Christ detailed in God's Word is unspeakably grand and self-evidently superb. The Bible paints the fullest display of the glory of God that we can see – for, in the Bible's revelation of Jesus Christ, we see God's glory in its brightest, fullest, most magnificent expression.

> For God, who commanded the light to shine out of darkness, hath shined in our hearts, to give

the light of the knowledge of the glory of God
in the face of Jesus Christ. (2 Corinthians 4:6)

As we celebrate the birth of Jesus Christ, we should take a minute to consider what is so triumphant about this particular celebration. Once upon a time, when Caesar Augustus decreed that all the world should be taxed, Mary and Joseph traveled to Joseph's ancestral home of Bethlehem, where Mary gave birth to God, veiled in human flesh. She laid Him in a manger; she wrapped Him in swaddling clothes; she fed Him, burped Him, changed His diaper, cooed at Him, and did everything we would expect a loving mother to do for her newborn baby. And this was God.

The God who framed the world entered it as an infant child, learned to talk and walk, had to be potty-trained, probably fell and scraped His knee, grew teeth, learned how to read and write, and matured from toddler to child to teenager to adult.[3]

And if you don't find that astounding enough, consider that during all the time of His infancy, during all His toddler years and childhood, this vulnerable child was Almighty God. Our sovereign God subjected Himself to His parents. The Provider and Sustainer of all things depended on Joseph to provide food and on Mary to feed Him.

Israel's religious establishment expected the Messiah to be one of them, or at least to approve of them. They expected Him to applaud them, to point out just how righteous and faithful they were. But they were wrong. And His refusal to pander to the powers that be demonstrates even more how glorious He was. They were the poison of Israel, and Jesus never tired of pointing it out. They sought approval from men, but Jesus was approved of God.

15

What baffled the religious ho-hums was that this man Jesus was from Nazareth, a lowly city in Galilee, the son of a carpenter. He never sat at their feet, never learned their ways, and never pretended that they were all that special. The people saw a profound difference between Christ and the scribes. His glory was self-attesting.

And why? Why should Jesus make Himself as fully a man as every other man? Why should He enter our world the way we did when He was the one who created our world? Why should He make Himself dependent on people He had Himself created? Why would Jesus associate with the lowest? Why would He become one of us?

The Bible speaks with clarity on this point.

> Forasmuch then as the children are partakers of flesh and blood, he also himself likewise took part of the same; that through death he might destroy him that had the power of death, that is, the devil; And deliver them who through fear of death were all their lifetime subject to bondage.

> Wherefore in all things it behoved him to be made like unto his brethren, that he might be a merciful and faithful high priest in things pertaining to God, to make reconciliation for the sins of the people. (Hebrews 2:14-15, 17)

The glory of Christ is the triumph of the skies. By faith, we can expect to join it!

# Reason #5: Because God Entered Our World

For God, who commanded the light to shine out
of darkness, hath shined in our hearts, to give
the light of the knowledge of the glory of God
in the face of Jesus Christ. (2 Corinthians 4:6)

The heavens declare the glory of God, and the great "triumph of the skies" is that the Maker of heaven and earth left the splendor of heaven to enter our world as a man. It astounds us to think that God would become what He made. The Creator made Himself into the creature – the thing He had created. If it weren't so familiar, it would surely overwhelm us.

John opens his gospel by pulling the curtain to show us before God's opening act that unrolled all His creative glory. Genesis 1:1 tells us, "In the beginning God created the heaven and the earth." That marks the beginning of history. John reveals what moderns would call "prehistoric" times, though they mean to deny the actual existence of God. Darwinists tell their fairy tales about cavemen and billions of years. They spin their alternate reality. So John reveals true reality in the first verse of his gospel, unveiling the eternity before the beginning of time. He tells us what was already there, already in place, already at work, in the beginning.

"In the beginning God created…" that is what God *did* at the beginning of time. But John wants us to look further back. He gives us a glimpse into infinity, into eternity past, when there was no time, no heaven and no earth, no world, no creation, only God. John tells us what was, already, when that moment of time began." "In the beginning was the Word." But the Word did not exist in a lifeless form or a zombie-like condition. John points us to eternity to show us the *beginning* of the beginning, the *life* of the beginning, the *cause* of the beginning.

John points us to Jesus. He was in the beginning, *with* God as distinct from the Father, while He at the same time *was* very God. He made all things without exception. He is the life of the world, and His life is the light of this world. And His life, which is the light of the world, invaded this world of darkness. Nor did the world of darkness comprehend it.

We know that this was Jesus because John does call Him by name. But before John uses His name in verse 17, he tells us something else we should know about Him.

> And the Word was made flesh, and dwelt among us, (and we beheld his glory, the glory as of the only begotten of the Father,) full of grace and truth.

Before the big reveal, John points to the Word and insists that He is God. He makes a shocking claim: the Word entered our world. He became one of us. And when we looked at Him, we saw God. John waits to reveal the true identity of the Word made flesh until he has completed this explanation of all that the Word is. Through this masterful introduction, John unveils the fulness of the glory of God in the face of Jesus Christ (Hebrews 1:3; 2 Corinthians 4:4-6; Colossians 1:15; Colossians 2:9).

But this is not just a glory to be *believed*. The glory of God entering our world blesses our lives. Because when God entered our world, He did not wield a sledgehammer above our heads. He did not brandish a sword, threatening to strike us down. He did not raise a hand against us (Isaiah 42:3; Matthew 12:20). He brought the solution to our problems. That solution was not something He carried, a cure that He delivered to us. That solution was His own self, the very person of Jesus Christ, the Word made flesh. He offered His own body in our place. That way, a man like us might be crucified for us.

Jesus made peace with God on our behalf. We offended God by our sin; Jesus satisfied God's righteous demands for justice when He died our death as our substitute.

In the Word made flesh, we see more clearly the triumph of the skies. And we are invited – this Christmas, every Christmas, and all the year round – to celebrate. When we pause to consider the lengths God went to so He could redeem us, it fills our hearts with joy and delight and adds barrels of life to our celebration of Christmas.

Join the triumph of the skies!

# Reason #6: Because He Was Born of a Virgin

> Therefore the Lord himself shall give you a sign;
> Behold, a virgin shall conceive, and bear a son,
> and shall call his name Immanuel. (Isaiah 7:14)

T hey say it isn't possible. It simply can't be. Phooey.
They say it should read "a young maiden," not a virgin.
They say, "There were many so-called virgin births in that backward time."

But God pledged it as a sign that He would deliver His people from the hands of Rezin, the king of Syria, and Pekah, the son of Remaliah, king of Israel. And God kept His promise.

> But while he thought on these things, behold, the angel of the Lord appeared unto him in a dream, saying, Joseph, thou son of David, fear not to take unto thee Mary thy wife: for that which is conceived in her is of the Holy Ghost. And she shall bring forth a son, and thou shalt call his name JESUS: for he shall save his people from their sins. Now all this was done, that it might be fulfilled which was spoken of the Lord by the prophet, saying, Behold, a virgin shall be with child, and shall bring forth a son, and they shall call his name Emmanuel, which being interpreted is, God with us. (Matthew 1:20-23)

God's people embrace the virgin birth. To deny it is to say, "I do not believe the Bible." Because the Bible plainly states that Mary would give birth to Jesus, having never known a man.

The virgin birth is both essential doctrine and manifestation of God's power over the natural world. Those who deny the virgin birth should admit that they reject all miracles. They deny the possibility of a God who intervenes in our world.

The glory of the Incarnation includes this extraordinary detail – that our Lord was conceived in a way no other man was. God made Himself a man, but the way He did it – the triumph of the skies – was by making a virgin womb the portal through which He entered our world.

Nobody should be surprised by this. A God who made everything from nothing and made the first man out of the dust of the ground won't struggle to make Himself a man. And the fact of His miraculous conception does not mean it was difficult or impossible.

The angel noted the significance of it. "That holy thing that shall be born of thee shall be called the Son of God." His enemies slandered Him, poisoning the well because of the scandal of His birth. But it matters that Jesus did not have an earthly father. He is the Son of God, not the Son of Adam. He is the man God sent to break the cycle of sin, to undo the Fall. He could not then be descended from Adam. He is the second Adam: able to do what Adam couldn't do – face temptation and overcome it.

Yet, we understand why unbelievers struggle to embrace such an unexpected fact. To admit the virgin birth is to acknowledge that Jesus Christ is a man unlike any other man, the kind of man who can save us. That is the glory of the virgin birth: when we embrace it, we must also embrace His deity. And as

Jesus is God, He alone is able to save us. He who admits the former must accept the latter. This is the glory of the Christmas story – the triumph of the skies. We urge you to join with that triumph, lest you instead be condemned with the world.

# Reason #7: Because He Made Himself of No Reputation

He is despised and rejected of men; a man of
sorrows, and acquainted with grief: and we hid
as it were our faces from him; he was despised,
and we esteemed him not. (Isaiah 53:3)

**M**atthew relates an event that startled the three eyewitnesses.
Six days earlier, Jesus had asked His disciples who men
said that He was. The disciples answered, "Some say that thou art
John the Baptist: some, Elias; and others, Jeremias, or one of the
prophets." Then, Jesus asked, "But whom say ye that I am?" Peter
piped up with an immediate answer: "Thou art the Christ, the Son
of the living God."

According to Matthew,

From that time forth began Jesus to shew unto his
disciples, how that he must go unto Jerusalem, and
suffer many things of the elders and chief priests
and scribes, and be killed, and be raised again the
third day. (Matthew 16:21)

The disciples did not respond well to this.

23

> Then Peter took him, and began to rebuke him,
> saying, Be it far from thee, Lord: this shall not be
> unto thee. But he turned, and said unto Peter, Get
> thee behind me, Satan: thou art an offence unto
> me: for thou savourest not the things that be of
> God, but those that be of men. (Matthew 16:22-23)

Matthew connects this conversation to the startling event on a high mountain six days later.

> And after six days Jesus taketh Peter, James, and
> John his brother, and bringeth them up into an
> high mountain apart, And was transfigured before
> them: and his face did shine as the sun, and his
> raiment was white as the light. (Matthew 17:1-2)

What amazed the three disciples was the contrast with Christ's normal appearance. Jesus was "transfigured" – that is, His outward expression changed so dramatically that, though He was still clearly recognized, the glory of His deity was for a moment put on full display before the disciples. Peter later described himself as being an "eyewitness of his majesty" (2 Peter 1:16)

> For he received from God the Father honour and
> glory, when there came such a voice to him from
> the excellent glory, This is my beloved Son, in
> whom I am well pleased. (2 Peter 1:17)

In His transfiguration, God unveiled for a moment the deity, the glory of Christ that was there all the time. As Charles Wesley teaches in his wonderful hymn, His Godhead was veiled in human flesh. Throughout His earthly life, Jesus

> …made himself of no reputation, and took upon him the form of a servant, and was made in the likeness of men: (Philippians 2:7)

Though Jesus emptied Himself, He did not empty Himself of His actual glory, the glory He shared with God the Father. The Mount of Transfiguration confirms this.

Paul reminds us that the glory of God shines brightest in the face of Jesus Christ.

> For God, who commanded the light to shine out of darkness, hath shined in our hearts, to give the light of the knowledge of the glory of God in the face of Jesus Christ. (2 Corinthians 4:6)

But the men of His day could not see this glory until after Jesus rose from the dead.

> And declared to be the Son of God with power, according to the spirit of holiness, by the resurrection from the dead: (Romans 1:4)

When Jesus "made Himself of no reputation," He emptied Himself – as Kenneth Wuest points out – of "self."[4] That is Paul's argument in Philippians 2:

> Let nothing be done through strife or vainglory; but in lowliness of mind let each esteem other

better than themselves. Look not every man on
his own things, but every man also on the things
of others. Let this mind be in you, which was also
in Christ Jesus: (Philippians 2:3-5)

The self He emptied was naturally much greater than the self
any of us possess. But Jesus did not think Himself robbed by the
nature He assumed. He made Himself of no reputation. Jesus had
the bearing of a slave. In this, He displayed His true purpose in
entering our world.

Even as the Son of man came not to be ministered
unto, but to minister, and to give his life a ransom
for many. (Matthew 20:28)

The pompous religious authorities were unprepared for
Jesus the Nazarene, the Galilean, the bondslave. They refused to
acknowledge Him as anything more than a carpenter's son, and
probably born of fornication.

But this is the triumph of the skies – that one so lowly should
be so exalted, that one who was so great made Himself so despised,
so He could elevate the despised and give them a share in His glory.

For ye know the grace of our Lord Jesus Christ,
that, though he was rich, yet for your sakes he
became poor, that ye through his poverty might
be rich. (2 Corinthians 8:9)

And this is the triumph of the skies, which we are privi-
leged to enjoy!

# Reason #8:  Because of His Unspeakable Gift

> But not as the offence, so also is the free gift.
> For if through the offence of one many be dead,
> much more the grace of God, and the gift by
> grace, which is by one man, Jesus Christ, hath
> abounded unto many. (Romans 5:15)

N othing builds anticipation for Christmas quite like presents. Gift-giving is one of our great Christmas traditions. It reminds us of the "unspeakable gift" of our Savior, Jesus Christ.

> For God so loved the world, that he gave his
> only begotten Son, that whosoever believeth in
> him should not perish, but have everlasting life.
> (John 3:16)

Our gift-giving tradition gives us a fantastic way to commemorate God's unspeakable gift, the gift of His Son.

In the world of nature, everything gives. The sun, moon, and stars give light. The earth yields fruit. Flowers give their fragrance and beauty. Grass gives its life to the animals. Animals give their service to men. The ocean gives water to the clouds. The clouds pour out their rain. The mountains give us streams to fill our lakes and reservoirs. The rivers and lakes and oceans give up their fish for mankind.

God made a giving world because He is a giving God. His giving surpasses the giving of His created world. God gives beauty to delight and truth to know and goodness to bless. And He gives Himself: the gift that outdoes any other giving in our world. Just as the sun outshines the moon and stars, so that in the daytime, the stars fade in the sun's superior light, so the giving of the natural world is all swallowed up in the self-giving of God.

God gave Himself in the Person of His Son Jesus Christ, the second Person of the Trinity. The babe in Bethlehem was not God the Father. God the Father gave us God the Son, "the Word made flesh." And the Incarnation is a gift. For in the Incarnation, God was not giving something He *had*. He was giving Himself – Who He *is*. The Father is not the Son, yet the Father and the Son are one God, "the same in essence, equal in power and glory." God gave Himself in the Person of His own dear Son. The Bible makes this abundantly clear in passages like Colossians 1:15, 2:9, Hebrews 1:3, I Timothy 3:16, and I Timothy 6:16.

God's giving of Himself is a priceless gift. The infinite God gave Himself – the Ancient of Days, the Almighty One, Sovereign Lord, Creator of all things, the Alpha and the Omega, Immortal, Eternal, the only wise God, King of Kings and Lord of Lords. He did not invent gifts to give us. He did not purchase His gifts for us. Instead, He gave His very Self in the Person of Christ.

This gift should inspire all our giving: the infant born in Bethlehem was the eternal God. Imagine those tiny fingers and toes, that crying baby, head wobbling, legs kicking, eyes looking but not exactly seeing. That babe in the manger is God. When God became one of us, He didn't make Himself a super baby; He didn't skip those early, awkward stages of human growth. Instead, the Incarnate God determined to become what we are. He willingly made Himself helpless, entirely dependent on another human being for support and sustenance. The fact of it should stun us – that the Son of God depended on a woman who relies utterly on Himself. The infinite God, the incarnate God, gave Himself in an indescribable gift of self-sacrifice.

Part of Christ's self-sacrifice included laying aside His glory and taking the form of a servant upon Himself. Part of His self-giving meant leaving the splendor of heaven and entering our world. Part of His self-giving included trading the reverence He enjoyed in heaven for the ridicule He endured on earth. It included the suffering He endured in our place, for our sin, as our substitute. Jesus died our death. He bore our sins and was forsaken by God the Father. Jesus dove deep to raise us high. He emptied Himself to fill us. He humbled Himself to exalt us.

Who could fully express all that Christ has done for us? Truly, it is an unspeakable gift. He has begotten us again to a lively hope, to an inheritance that is incorruptible and undefiled and that fadeth not away. Those who receive Him as Savior are accepted in the beloved, at one with God, reconciled. We have redemption and peace and rest and life and hope by the gift of God through Jesus Christ. What more can we say? God gives the gift freely. God Himself gives the gift. God Himself is the gift.

It is an unspeakable gift – words cannot fully convey all that is given in our Savior. The giving of the gift is unspeakable. The value of the gift is immeasurable. The cost of the gift is immense.

> Forasmuch as ye know that ye were not
> redeemed with corruptible things, as silver and
> gold, from your vain conversation received by
> tradition from your fathers; But with the pre-
> cious blood of Christ, as of a lamb without
> blemish and without spot: (I Peter 1:18-19)

We cannot measure the benefits of the gift. This gift grants the believer repentance of sin, forgiveness of sins, eternal life, rest, hope, peace, and victory.

And the blessings of these gifts are boundless. Christ delivers us from the harmful effects and the powerful influence of our sins. God gives inward peace. We enjoy fellowship with God. We have joy. Jesus removes the enmity between God and us so we can delight in Him and find satisfaction.

God's unspeakable gift provides us with two ways to "join the triumph of the skies" this Christmas. First, we should wit- ness. Go tell it. Paul calls it the "unspeakable gift:" that is, the gift that cannot be fully told. But we should tell it and tell it everywhere. Gratitude should flavor our gospel witness. Second, we should imitate God by giving good gifts and giving a little of ourselves in each of our gifts. We are never more like our Savior than when we give ourselves in self-sacrifice.

# Reason #9:  Because Angels Announced His Birth

And without controversy great is the mystery of
godliness: God was manifest in the flesh, justified in the Spirit, seen of angels, preached unto
the Gentiles, believed on in the world, received
up into glory. (I Timothy 3:16)

Manger scenes usually include an angel somewhere in
the mix. The angel in the package might provoke our
inner curmudgeon because said angel doesn't much resemble
the ones described in Scripture. Nativity scene angels tend to
be beautiful women with pleasing, kindly features and perhaps
a beautiful golden trumpet. Such an angel is not to be found in
the Bible. In the Bible, a lone angel killed 185,000 Assyrians in
a single night (2 Kings 19:35). Think about that: in the deadliest
battle in United States history (Gettysburg), close to 51,000 soldiers died over a three-day period. On the bloodiest single day
in American history (Antietam), nearly 23,000 soldiers died.
A solitary angel on a single night killed 185,000 men without
raising much of a fuss.

When King David sinned in numbering the people, another
lone angel destroyed 70,000 men from Dan to Beersheba and
then stretched out his hand upon Jerusalem to destroy it. Only
the command of the Lord stayed the angel's hand (2 Samuel
24:15-16). No wonder when an angel appeared in the Bible, he
tended to greet people with "Fear not." The visit of a Biblical

31

angel doesn't resemble anything in a Hallmark movie, in other words. The appearance of an angel threw men into a panic.

So, the angels who announced the birth of Christ looked nothing like the pudgy toddlers or girlish Victorians in our modern nativity scenes. The Bible tells us that when the angels visited the shepherds, they were "sore afraid" – literally, they "feared a great fear." They were terrified.

Shepherds weren't exactly wilting or timid souls. They were more on the rowdy side – ancient rednecks. They lived outdoors, fought off predators, and faced their share of danger in the wild. The sight of angels filling the night sky caused these rough and ready men to shrink in fear.

> And the angel said unto them, Fear not: for, behold, I bring you good tidings of great joy, which shall be to all people. (Luke 2:10)

The angels announced the kind of news that no mere mortal would be fit to tell. It was heavenly news, the best news, for the Creator God invaded our world that very night. How right that a terrifying host of angels should serve as the heralds of this good news.

When the angel announced his good news, he didn't offer it as a suggestion that the shepherds might find interesting. He didn't advertise it like a TV special. The angel's message was good for the world, and he announced it as if the world needed to know.

> For unto you is born this day in the city of David a Saviour, which is Christ the Lord. (Luke 2:11)

Let skeptics sulk and Rabbis rant. The angel had a message, and he delivered it with force. It was good news – good tidings of great joy which shall be to all people. The angels evangelized the shepherds – the Greek word rendered "good tidings." They preached the gospel. A Savior is born this very day. Caesar Augustus (ironically) fancied himself a savior, but he delivered more people to death than he did to life, and in the end, he couldn't save himself. The only Savior is Christ the Lord. A little earlier, another angel instructed Joseph to "call his name JESUS, for he shall save his people from their sins."

Consider the gospel according to angels: the Savior was born at a particular time, on a particular day in history. He is a real person, born in a real place, and He made a real way for you to come to God. For He is born "unto you." Not to the elites. Not to the religious. Not to the moral. Neither to the rich and powerful nor the poor and insignificant. Jesus was not born "unto" an exclusive group of people. The angel addressed his "unto you" to shepherds in their field. But the gospel is "to all people." Shepherds would assume they were excluded if the announcement came to the elites first. By announcing to the shepherds first, God sent a clear message: this is good news for the despised and excluded. That way, we would know this is good news for us.

But the angel didn't expect the shepherds to take his word for it. He gave them proof.

> And this shall be a sign unto you; Ye shall find
> the babe wrapped in swaddling clothes, lying in
> a manger. (Luke 2:12)

He provided a sign, a means by which they would know it was true. God gives us every reason to believe what the Bible says about Christ; the most compelling reason may be the sign itself. The angel didn't leave a trail of cookie crumbs for the shepherds to follow. Instead, he gave a sign. What was the sign? A real baby. Like any other baby born then, the baby's mother swaddled Him. They would find the babe lying in a manger, which told them to look in a stable. Besides the stable, nothing unusual. The sign that confirmed the angel's message as good news for the world was that an ordinary baby was born in a stable in Bethlehem.

Lo and behold, the shepherds found Jesus precisely the way the angels said they would. And if you will seek Jesus, you will find Him too, just as the Bible says. Herein lies the triumph of the skies – ordinary sinners like you and like me can come to this same Jesus, the one born in Bethlehem, wrapped in swaddling clothes, lying in a manger, and we can receive Him, be redeemed from all our sin, and be reconciled to God.

Hallelujah! What a Savior!

# Reason #10:  Because Hallmark Doesn't Get All the Fun

The Spirit of the Lord is upon me, because he hath anointed me to preach the gospel to the poor; he hath sent me to heal the brokenhearted, to preach deliverance to the captives, and recovering of sight to the blind, to set at liberty them that are bruised, (Luke 4:18)

I s your name Chrissy-Ann Cringle, but people just call you Chris? Are you a busy New York City executive with more money than you can spend but no social life? Have you recently moved to your small hometown in New England in search of meaning and, perhaps, love? Then welcome, my friend, to Hallmark, New Hampshire, home of the world's oldest living Christmas tree.

After all, how could we discuss the holidays and ignore this favorite, slightly cringy holiday tradition? Off the record, I count it a mark of God's special favor to me that my wife doesn't like Hallmark movies. I can tolerate a lady who enjoys them, but a man who likes Hallmark movies? As they say in Denmark, "Egad!"

If I enter a store with a Hallmark movie playing, I clutch my man card and hurry out. I think I hear the Wuss train clanging its little Tinker bell and chugging into the station, and I refuse to get on board. If you wanted to tailor the most horrific torture session for me, lock me in a room with a Hallmark movie playing, and no remote. I think I feel brain cells dying off even now – a regular genocide of gray matter dying under the most painful circumstances.

Are spoiler alerts possible for Hallmark movies? But they do explain Prince Harry and Meghan Markle. You know the difference between a True Crime story and a Hallmark movie, right? In the True Crime story, the handsome stranger never learns the true meaning of Christmas. So, what has fifteen actors, four settings, two writers, and one plot? 632 Hallmark movies.

I don't argue that Christmas is overly commercialized. I do, however, argue that Christmas is overly *romanticized*. Blame it on the myth that a mug of hot cocoa and a Botox treatment can fix life's problems. Nothing like gently falling snow and Christmas lights to solve all our family problems. Of course, it does help if the handsome guy in the designer flannel shirt happens to be fabulously wealthy, especially if that is the worst-kept secret in the show.

But enough mockery. If a point is to be made here, I suppose we should make it. Hallmark movies have other reasons for their popularity besides the wussification of the American male. Fundamentally, God created the world a certain way, with native passions common to mankind in our fallen state. Hallmark Holidays show the reality of our messed-up lives and our longing for someone to rescue us from it. This universal longing for rescue explains why the Hallmark formula works and why there can be more than a thousand movies with one plot and variations on the same actors. Because ultimately, everyone wants to live happily ever after.

We like the predictability of the Hallmark plot. We find it comforting that, in the end, everything will be made right again and people will find "the true meaning of Christmas" (I doubt Hallmark gets that right, but you know what I mean). We long for the certainty, the comfort, the hope that a Hallmark movie promises.

Hallmark movies vaguely imitate the gospel's impact on a person's messed-up life. The gospel is very predictable this way. The gospel brings order to the chaos, repairs the ruins of the Fall, and fills the heart with joy, peace, and satisfaction – all things that Hallmark movies pretend to do.

But in light of God's Word, we find no comparison between the gospel and a Hallmark movie. Because a Hallmark movie acts as if our problems can be solved by a romantic encounter, a few more self-serving decisions, or some human invention apart from Jesus Christ. And we should know how that goes.

Suppose we made a sequel to any given Hallmark movie, a sort of "two years later" when the magic of romance has worn off, and the sinful ways of the main characters have caught up to the story. Now what? Maybe things can end as badly in those stories as they do in real life.

Only Christ, through His redemptive power, can heal the brokenness caused by sin. The gospel of Jesus Christ alone can forever heal the hurt in your heart. Only Jesus brings lasting peace.

You can be forgiven if you like to watch a Hallmark movie at this time of year. I won't judge you too harshly. Just don't invite me to join you. But as you watch, I hope you will remember that what Hallmark pretends to do, Jesus does. And what He does far surpasses any Hallmark Holiday.

This, my friend, is the triumph of the skies: that there is nothing like it in the world – no comparison we can make to the power and sufficiency of the grace of God that brings salvation. Thanks be unto God for His unspeakable gift!

# Reason #11: Because Jesus is God's Greatest Expression of Love

> For God so loved the world, that he gave his
> only begotten Son, that whosoever believeth in
> him should not perish, but have everlasting life.
> (John 3:16)

T he Bible gives several beautiful summaries of the gospel,
none more eloquent than John 3:16. "For God so loved the
world…." The "for" gives a reason: "'because' God so loved
the world," pointing back to what was said about Moses lifting
up the serpent in the wilderness:

> And as Moses lifted up the serpent in the wil-
> derness, even so must the Son of man be lifted
> up: (John 3:14)

The Son of man must be lifted up *because* God so loved the
world. The cross is the purpose of Christ's coming. We cannot
speak rightly of the newborn King, the babe born at Bethlehem,
and ignore the cross as the central reason and ultimate purpose
for His birth. And though we enjoy the message of "peace on
earth" at Christmastime, we must not forget that this peace
came at a great price. Therefore, our Christmas celebration
should keep the cruel torture of the cross in view.

> Therefore doth my Father love me, because
> I lay down my life, that I might take it again.
> No man taketh it from me, but I lay it down of
> myself. I have power to lay it down, and I have
> power to take it again. This commandment have
> I received of my Father. (John 10:17-18)

The Son of man must be lifted up. Apart from the cross, the birth of Jesus is just one birth among many on that first Christmas night. Without the cross, Jesus is just another man, a liar as it turns out, running the biggest hoax in history. Jesus must be lifted up on the cross. That is His purpose in entering our world.

> And I, if I be lifted up from the earth, will draw
> all men unto me. (John 12:32)

The Bible gives this purpose for the cross: "That whosoever believeth in him should not perish, but have eternal life" (John 3:15). Why will believers have eternal life?

> For (because) God so loved the world, that he
> gave his only begotten Son (John 3:16).

Why must the Son of man be lifted up on the cross? Because God so loved the world. He loved the world so much that He gave His only begotten Son. He gave the unspeakable gift, which can never be fully described or told. And His purpose in this gift of all gifts? "That whosoever believeth in him should not perish, but have everlasting life."

But there is more. Why won't believers perish? "For God sent not his Son into the world to condemn the world; but that the world through him might be saved" (John 3:17). Everything traces back to God's declaration of love to the world. When God announced His love to mankind, He said it in a Person: The Word – The Expression (if you will) – made flesh. Jesus is God's love note to the world.

But we shouldn't think of this in romantic terms, as if God saw a beautiful, attractive, desirable world and "set His cap" for it. God's declaration of love stands out from any other in history because He gave it to as undeserving a race of people (the world) that ever existed: people who did not deserve it and did not want it. When John speaks of the world, he stresses the world's rebellion against God in the form of lust and sin. In John's first epistle, he forbids us from loving the world.

> Love not the world, neither the things that are in the world. If any man love the world, the love of the Father is not in him. For all that is in the world, the lust of the flesh, and the lust of the eyes, and the pride of life, is not of the Father, but is of the world. (I John 2:15-16)

How can God love the world when He forbids us to love the world? This is no trick question. God forbids our delighting in the things the world enjoys or participating with it in its self-will and lust-driven rebellion.[5] God takes no pleasure in the sin and rebellion of the world, which makes His expression of love at Christmas so staggering. God is "angry with the wicked every day." And yet, He loves the world. Sin provides the back-drop that displays God's amazing love for the world.

> But God commendeth his love toward us, in
> that, while we were yet sinners, Christ died for
> us. (Romans 5:8)

The cross offers the most vivid display of love ever seen. Jesus must be crucified because God loves the world. God gave His one and only Son so that whoever believed in Him should not perish but have everlasting life.

We get warm, sentimental feelings about nativity scenes. But let us not forget that the true glory, the great triumph of the scene, shows up at the end of the babe's life. As religious authorities rail against Him and scream for His blood, as officers hand Him over for crucifixion, as soldiers nail His hands and feet to the cross, as He bleeds and dies bearing the sin of the whole world, Jesus triumphs over the world. On the cross, Jesus defeated sin and hatred, death and Hell and Satan. And this is the most glorious piece of news you will ever hear.

> Fear not: for, behold, I bring you good tidings of
> great joy, which shall be to all people. For unto
> you is born this day in the city of David a Saviour,
> which is Christ the Lord. (Luke 2:10-11)

# Reason #12:  Because He Was Announced to Shepherds

> And there were in the same country shepherds
> abiding in the field, keeping watch over their
> flock by night. And, lo, the angel of the Lord
> came upon them, and the glory of the Lord
> shone round about them: and they were sore
> afraid. And the angel said unto them, Fear not:
> for, behold, I bring you good tidings of great
> joy, which shall be to all people. For unto you
> is born this day in the city of David a Saviour,
> which is Christ the Lord. (Luke 2:8-11)

Think of the joy of a newborn baby. The parents can't
wait to show their new baby to the world. Typically, we
announce the good news to our closest friends and immediate
family first. Then, we pass the word around the church. Next,
phone calls and text messages spread the message. These days,
a Facebook announcement is sure to follow, with plenty of
pictures. Parents want their family and friends to know they
have a new child.

So, we may find it curious that when God announced the
birth of His Son, He didn't tell it first to the chief priests or
Pharisees. We suspect that the religious authorities in Israel
may have expected to be first in line for the newsflash. After
all, wouldn't God want them to know? Were they not the fore-
most authorities in all things related to the Messiah? Herod

acknowledged their expertise. The magi put Jerusalem in an uproar with their question, "Where is he that is born King of the Jews?" Herod knew who to ask. He sent for the doctors of the law.

These doctors must have expected the Messiah would be one of them. At least, He should recognize their deep devotion, holding them up as an example and honoring them before the people (see John 5:40-44). Maybe that explains why they didn't bother to travel the five miles to Bethlehem to see the baby Jesus for themselves, though they could tell the wise men where to find Him.

God didn't announce the birth of Jesus to the religious authorities. Nor did He announce His birth to the royalty of that day. Caesar Augustus didn't get a message, as far as we know. King Herod got the word second-hand through the visiting magi. The wise men didn't get the memo either but learned the news from a star. Surely, the king deserved to hear the word directly from God, not second-hand from foreign wise men.

But God didn't announce the birth of Jesus to the rich, the powerful, the important, or the wise. He didn't announce it to the nation of Israel, or the city of Jerusalem, or the people of Bethlehem. Big cities like Jerusalem may feel a sense of self-importance, but God did not feed that conceit.

The angels announced the birth of Jesus to shepherds. Does that strike us as odd? We can't say why God wanted the shepherds to know. Alfred Edersheim believed that this particular crew of shepherds cared for the temple flock, the sheep destined for sacrifice at the temple.[6] He suggested that God wanted these shepherds to know that the final lamb, the

Lamb of God that takes away the sins of the world, was just now born. That could be.

But the Bible doesn't explain God's choice of shepherds for the announcement. We know that every patriarch of Israel had been a shepherd. Abel was a shepherd. Abraham was a shepherd. Jacob was a shepherd. Moses was a shepherd. David was the most famous shepherd of all. Yet, by the time Jesus was born, much of the shine had worn off that particular occupation. People didn't think very highly of a shepherd. They belonged on the lower rungs of the social ladder. We could compare them to a modern-day construction crew, hard-working, hard-living, swearing, fighting, and hardly fit for high society. So the angels probably didn't interrupt the shepherd's devotion time when they announced the good news that Jesus was born.

> And there were in the same country shepherds
> abiding in the field, keeping watch over their
> flock by night. (Luke 2:8)

The shepherds were doing what shepherds do, in other words. God gave the good news to working men doing their job.

Can we take away a little something from this? Society might frown on you. The "elites" might despise your particular occupation and make superficial judgments about you. But God honored hard-working men, maybe a little rough around the edges, with the most significant piece of breaking news the world has ever received. God honored shepherds in their calling.

Let that encourage you to go about your work, serving the Lord in whatever you do. Remember the way God chooses the foolish things of the world to confound the wise, the weak things to confound the mighty, the base things, the despised, the things that are not, to bring to nought things that are: "That no flesh should glory in his presence" (I Corinthians 1:27-29).

And this, too, is the triumph of the skies.

# Reason #13:  Because Wise Men Celebrated Christmas

> Now when Jesus was born in Bethlehem of
> Judaea in the days of Herod the king, behold,
> there came wise men from the east to Jerusalem,
> Saying, Where is he that is born King of the
> Jews? for we have seen his star in the east, and
> are come to worship him. (Matthew 2:1-2)

L et yourself be surprised by the wonder of the wise men.
Here are a few points that might astonish us.

First, nothing in the gospel record suggests that these
men were kings. The King James Bible calls them wise men.
The Greek word is *magi*, the Persian term for a "magician"
or "astrologer." We sing "We Three Kings" at Christmastime,
assuming there was one wise man per gift. Someone suggested
that they could just as well have been six, one for each end of
the gifts.[7] These wealthy Gentile dignitaries from the "East"
came to worship the newborn King.

Second, they traveled many miles to worship the Messiah.
But the Jewish religious authorities couldn't travel a few miles
to see the long-expected Jesus. They knew the prophets well
enough that they could pronounce where the Messiah would be
born. But they couldn't go to Bethlehem to see the baby Jesus
for themselves.

Third, the wise men entered Jerusalem with a question:

> Where is he that is born King of the Jews? For
> we have seen his star in the east, and are come
> to worship Him.

God was behind this question, for God wanted specific people to hear about this birth. So, God brought it to Herod's attention. Their question startled a very paranoid usurper of Israel's throne – a king who needed troubling. All Jerusalem was troubled, though for a different reason than Herod. Jerusalem's entire pack of apathetic religious posers also deserved a little hassle.

Fourth, God guided the wise men with a star. The Bible doesn't say exactly how they knew from a star that a king was born in Israel. Douglas Wilson suggests that they knew of Balaam, the Gentile prophet.[8] When a sovereign God compelled Balaam to bless instead of curse, his blessing promised "a Star out of Jacob."

> I shall see him, but not now: I shall behold him,
> but not nigh: there shall come a Star out of
> Jacob, and a Sceptre shall rise out of Israel, and
> shall smite the corners of Moab, and destroy all
> the children of Sheth. (Numbers 24:17)

Did these wise men know Balaam's prophecy? Perhaps it was recorded in other places besides the book of Numbers. Maybe they recognized its fulfillment, not only in the star they saw but also in Israel's current state of affairs. Balaam's prophecy included an announcement of judgment on Edom, and at that time, an Idumean (Herod) sat on Israel's throne.

> And Edom shall be a possession, Seir also shall
> be a possession for his enemies; and Israel shall
> do valiantly. Out of Jacob shall come he that
> shall have dominion, and shall destroy him that
> remaineth of the city. (Numbers 24:18-19)

We cannot say how the star communicated or how the wise men received that communication. Nor can we explain how it "stood over where the young child was." How does a star stand over a home?

Alpha Centauri, the nearest star besides earth's sun, is 4.4 light years away. A twinkle from that star takes nearly four and a half years to reach our eyes. One scientific source defines stars as great exploding balls of gas, made of helium and hydrogen. And though some stars are smaller than our sun (Proxima Centauri is about 1/8 the sun's mass), we can't imagine something even as small as the moon entering our atmosphere. A tiny comet might cause significant damage to our world.

How could this star stand over the place where the Lord was? Is this not a miracle? Wilson argues that we have to see it as miraculous either way we look at it.[9] Either the wise men "miraculously" calculated the location of the star so accurately that they could find the very house where Jesus was (a miracle of science), or else the star stood over the same house where Jesus was (a miracle of God). Those who rest in the authority of science will believe that the wise men did fantastic work with the Pythagorean Theorem. They will deny the possibility of a star entering our atmosphere, not because of a lack of evidence but because their doctrinal commitments won't allow it. Yet, the proof of a star entering our atmosphere is simply overwhelming. The wise men found the babe. They didn't go door to door and didn't have a star-gazer app on their smartphones.[10]

God has made some pretty remarkable things in our world, and the truth is, we don't know as much about the material substance of the things in this world as we might like to think. For example, science may know the material substance of a star. But science can't say what a star is.[11] So, we shouldn't find it remarkable that God would make a star enter our atmosphere to guide a caravan of magi from the east to a specific house in Bethlehem. The star isn't even the greatest miracle He performed on the first Christmas. It merely points to the greatest miracle He performed.

If you think it impossible that God would make a gas giant enter our atmosphere, consider this: The infinite God, Who can't be contained in the heavens or the heaven of heavens, made Himself the smallest, weakest, most helpless of all the creatures He created: a newborn babe. And in that babe, we see the substance of our triumph!

# Reason #14:  Because Mary Rejoiced

The mother of Jesus took great delight in joining the triumph of the skies. The Bible records her psalm of praise, and we are deeply enriched by the soul-rejoicing of "a mother's deep prayer." Mary tells us why we should praise the Word of God Incarnate with the angels. Notice her reasons:

> And Mary said, My soul doth magnify the Lord, And my spirit hath rejoiced in God my Saviour. For he hath regarded the low estate of his handmaiden: for, behold, from henceforth all generations shall call me blessed. For he that is mighty hath done to me great things; and holy is his name. And his mercy is on them that fear him from generation to generation. He hath shewed strength with his arm; he hath scattered the proud in the imagination of their hearts. He hath put down the mighty from their seats, and exalted them of low degree. He hath filled the hungry with good things; and the rich he hath sent empty away. He hath holpen his servant Israel, in remembrance of his mercy; As he spake to our fathers, to Abraham, and to his seed for ever. (Luke 1:46-55)

First, Mary gave a joyful word. She magnified the Lord in her soul; her spirit rejoiced in God her Savior. She did not magnify herself, by the way. Nor should we. But Mary recognized the unique blessing God gave her.

> For, behold, from henceforth all generations
> shall call me blessed. For he that is mighty hath
> done to me great things; and holy is his name.

Mary knew that God's special favor on her extended beyond her role in the birth of the Messiah. As a sinner, Mary was about to give birth to her own Savior.

Second, Mary gave a reasonable word. She gives four reasons why her soul magnified and her spirit rejoiced: first, because "he hath regarded the low estate of his handmaiden;" second, because "from henceforth all generations shall call me blessed;" third, because "he that is mighty hath done to me great things; and holy is his name;" fourth, because "his mercy is on them that fear him from generation to generation."

Third, Mary gave a militant word. She recognized God's offensive against sin in the announcement of this birth.

> He hath shewed strength with his arm; he hath
> scattered the proud in the imagination of their
> hearts. He hath put down the mighty from their
> seats, and exalted them of low degree.

Mary saw her own role in this assault. The seed of the woman was about to crush the serpent's head.

Fourth, Mary gave a grateful word. Gratitude fills this psalm to overflowing.

> He hath put down the mighty from their seats,
> and exalted them of low degree. He hath filled
> the hungry with good things; and the rich he
> hath sent empty away. He hath holpen his ser-
> vant Israel, in remembrance of his mercy.

Mary spoke of God's faithfulness (v. 48), power (v. 49), holiness (v. 49), and mercy (v. 50).[12] But she also recognized God's special favor on Israel in sending His Son into the world. She knew her Bible, and she understood that this birth fulfilled the covenant promises God made to Abraham and to his seed. In other words, her faith rested in the Word of God above the word of the angel. Mary was a woman of faith. She believed what the angel said because she believed what the Word of God said. So, not only was she a woman of faith, but she was a woman of the Word.

Fifth, Mary gave a prophetic word. Her psalm of praise burns with prophetic fire. Consider the way she predicts her son's coming greatness. Her psalm takes on a triumphant note; her words are all aglow with prophetic zeal

Finally, Mary gave a personal word. She had first-hand knowledge that God exalted them of low degree – because He had regarded the low estate of His handmaiden.

> For he that is mighty hath done to me great
> things; and holy is his name.

The Bible rarely uses generalities when praising God. We don't often get a "Lord, thank you for this day, thank you for everything you do." The Psalms are rich in particulars; they give a detailed account of why we should praise the Lord.

As we join the triumph of the skies, we ought to say with the angels, "Glory to God in the highest." But we should also take note of the staggering details of God's blessing on us. For He has given Himself for our sakes, entered our world as the lowest of us to raise sinners to heights of glory beyond our reach. He has not dealt with us according to our sins but has been merciful and gracious, forgiving iniquity and transgression and sin. He will by no means clear the guilty, yet He lays our sins on His own Son. He has so loved the world that He gave His only begotten Son, and whosoever believeth on Him shall not perish, but have everlasting life. Follow Mary's example: praise God in meaningful ways this Christmas.

# Reason #15:  Because He Has a Name Above All Names

> And being found in fashion as a man, he humbled himself, and became obedient unto death, even the death of the cross. Wherefore God also hath highly exalted him, and given him a name which is above every name: That at the name of Jesus every knee should bow, of things in heaven, and things in earth, and things under the earth; And that every tongue should confess that Jesus Christ is Lord, to the glory of God the Father. (Philippians 2:8-11)

B ecause of the perfect obedience of Jesus Christ, God highly exalted Him, giving Him a name above every name. His great name gives us good reason to celebrate Christmas. Every name of Jesus is as rich and meaningful and important and glorious as the next. So let's take a few moments to praise His names.

Isaiah called Him "Wonderful, Counsellor, The mighty God, The everlasting Father, The Prince of Peace" (Isaiah 9:6). His name is *Wonderful,* beyond expression, indescribably glorious. He is the Wonderful *Counselor* standing by us, defending us, guiding us, instructing us, and He has a glorious purpose for us. Jesus, *the mighty God,* fulfills all that glorious purpose toward us. Jesus *the everlasting Father* fathers us as the fount of our life and godliness. He is *the Prince of Peace.* He made peace for us and extended peace to us so that He could end our war with our Creator.

He is *Immanuel* – God with us. The face God presented to the world is the face of Jesus of Nazareth. In Jesus, God is with us, not against us. God the Father reconciles mankind to Himself in the person of God the Son.

Jesus is the *Word*, God's self-disclosure to the world. He is a kind Word, a compassionate Word, a gracious Word from the Father. He brings salvation to the world rather than judgment and condemnation for the world.

He is both *Son of God* and *Son of Man*. As the Son of God, He displayed His deity and holiness. This display of glory provoked deadly malice against Him. As the Son of Man, He has been given

> dominion, and glory, and a kingdom, that all people, nations, and languages, should serve him: his dominion is an everlasting dominion, which shall not pass away, and his kingdom that which shall not be destroyed. (Daniel 7:14)

Jesus is the *Messiah* – the one God anointed to bear our sins, to die our death, and to be the sacrifice for our sins that God would accept. He is the *Savior*, the One who brings salvation to the world. He is the *Nazarene* (Matthew 2:23). He made Himself an ordinary man, native to one of the most despised places in Israel, so that He could extend salvation to the lowest of us.

But of all His names, without a doubt, the most beloved is *Jesus*.

> And she shall bring forth a son, and thou shalt
> call his name JESUS: for he shall save his
> people from their sins. (Matthew 1:21)

Jesus is His common name, His given name. Jesus is the name we know, the name His friends use. From the time we learned about salvation, the name of Jesus became most precious to us.

> Neither is there salvation in any other: for there
> is none other name under heaven given among
> men, whereby we must be saved. (Acts 4:12)

That name, *Jesus*, makes Him real and personal and familiar. We look to Jesus; we pray in His name; we hope in Jesus; we rest on Jesus.

But "Jesus" was a common name in His lifetime. Josephus, the historian, mentions a dozen different men with that name. We find the name "Jesus" used several times in the Old Testament (Hosea and Joshua, for instance) and at least one other time in the New Testament.

Nor did Jesus have a good name in His day – at least among His rivals. Adversaries called Him gluttonous and a winebibber, a friend of publicans and sinners. They said He was "born of fornication." They called Him a blasphemer. Nevertheless, Jesus embraced this "bad" name, laying aside His glorious reputation to enter our world and save us from our sins (Philippians 2:7).

Why call Him Jesus? The angel explains: "For he shall save his people from their sins." His reason is worth considering. First, "He shall save." Jesus Himself meets our most profound need. He offers us salvation. We find a promise of this in His very name: He shall *save* – that is, Jesus makes "his soul an offering for our sins."

> For he hath made him to be sin for us, who knew no sin; that we might be made the righteousness of God in him. (2 Corinthians 5:21)

Second, "He shall save *his people.*" Not the Jews only, for many have rejected Jesus. Not the worthy, because nobody would qualify. Jesus came to save sinners. He doesn't reward people for their righteousness; He saves them from their sins. Not our goodness but our badness qualifies us for His salvation.

"His people" believe that Jesus is the only hope for salvation and trust Him for it. "His people" come to Him with their sins. In return, Jesus comes to save you, not to admire you. He comes to forgive you, not to reward you.

If you think you have no need for this, then you are not one of "His" people. And Jesus only saves His *people.* Jesus saves real people with real sins and real guilt who feel a real sense of condemnation for their sins and a real sense of need for Jesus.

Finally, Jesus saves people *from their sins.* The physician helps the sick, not the healthy. So, Jesus has nothing for the righteous. But Jesus brings sinners to repentance, ending the penalty and power of sin, teaching them to live free from sin's presence.

This is the triumph of the skies: Jesus came into the world to save sinners. And as always, you are warmly encouraged to join it!

# Reason #16: Because Great Is the Mystery of Godliness

> And without controversy great is the mystery of
> godliness: God was manifest in the flesh, justi-
> fied in the Spirit, seen of angels, preached unto
> the Gentiles, believed on in the world, received
> up into glory. (I Timothy 3:16)

J esus entered our world for a higher purpose than saving us
from hell. He came to make us holy. Paul invites us to consider "the mystery of *godliness*" – how God transforms a sinner
into a saint. Piety poses a great mystery. We cannot dispute it.

What is the mystery of godliness? *God was manifest in the
flesh, justified in the Spirit, seen of angels, preached unto the
Gentiles, believed on in the world, received up into glory.*

Paul tacks this note of praise to the end of a passage
describing the qualifications of the pastor and deacons. In that
passage, Paul raised the standard high – some might say impos-
sibly high. Paul doesn't disagree. How can those who once
lived according to the lusts of their flesh and of their minds be
so transformed as to be called "godly"?

In answer, Paul points us to the birth of Jesus. He provides
us with three contrasts and three parallels to help us remember
how God transforms us. We will look past the poetic features
of this ancient hymn to see the glory of God's grace at work in
the Christian's life.

Adam's sin ruined God's image in us. Jesus came as a Second Adam to do what the first Adam could not. He successfully resisted Satan's temptations; He perfectly obeyed God's law. In His death, He fully paid the penalty for our sin, delivered the believer from its bondage, and began the glorious process of delivering His people from sin's presence. Great is this mystery of godliness!

Paul offers six ways a man is re-made, restored, renewed, and renovated into the image of Christ. First, we become Christ-like by the Incarnation of Jesus Christ. "God was manifest in the flesh." He made Himself like us so we can be made like Him. He transforms us by causing us to see God in the face of Jesus Christ.

> But we all, with open face beholding as in a glass the glory of the Lord, are changed into the same image from glory to glory, even as by the Spirit of the Lord. (2 Corinthians 3:18)

Second, a man becomes Christ-like by the resurrection of Jesus Christ. He was "justified in the Spirit." A sinner is justified by a legal declaration of "not guilty" – not because we aren't guilty, but because God transfers our guilt to Jesus. Jesus needs no justification from sin. For Him, "justified" means that He is proven or vindicated. His resurrection proves His qualification to be our Savior.

> And **declared** to be the Son of God with power, according to the spirit of holiness, by the resurrection from the dead: (Romans 1:4)

That which justifies Jesus justifies us.

> Now it was not written for his sake alone, that
> it was imputed to him; But for us also, to whom
> it shall be imputed, if we believe on him that
> raised up Jesus our Lord from the dead; Who
> was delivered for our offences, *and was raised
> again for our justification.* (Romans 4:23-25)

The same Spirit that raised Jesus from the dead raises us out
of death to walk in newness of life. In this, we see the power
of the gospel at work in our lives.

> And what is *the exceeding greatness of his
> power **to** us-ward who believe,* according to
> the working of his mighty power, Which he
> wrought in Christ, when he raised him from the
> dead, and set him at his own right hand in the
> heavenly places, (Ephesians 1:19-20)

Third, Jesus was seen of angels. How can that affect our
sanctification? Peter says that angels desire to look into these
things (I Peter 1:12). Apparently, they find it a great mystery
as well, this marvelous transformation of a believer. What do
angels see when they look? Not propositions. Not abstractions.
Not points of doctrine. They see Jesus. They witness the trans-
forming godliness of a believer through Christ. They look at the
believer, and they see Jesus at work. Angels know the answer
to the mystery when they see Jesus.[13]

> **Wherefore** gird up the loins of your mind, be
> sober, and hope to the end for the grace that
> is to be brought unto you *at the revelation of*
> *Jesus Christ*; As obedient children, not fash-
> ioning yourselves according to the former lusts
> in your ignorance: But as he which hath called
> you is holy, so be ye holy in all manner of con-
> versation; Because it is written, Be ye holy; for
> I am holy. (I Peter 1:13-16)

The fourth part of the mystery of godliness is that Christ was
"preached unto the Gentiles." God chose the "foolishness of
preaching" as the means of conversion and Christ-likeness. The
preaching of the gospel changes us, making us new creatures.

The fifth part of the "mystery of godliness" is that Christ is
"believed on in the world." And on this, I will let Spurgeon speak:

> The mystery is not that Christ is served in the
> world, that is not put here; not that Christ is wor-
> shipped in the world, that is not the first point
> — those things will be sure to follow: but the
> vital mystery is that Christ is "believed on in
> the world," that is to say, trusted as the Savior.[14]

Paul identifies a sixth part of the mystery that transforms
the believer: Jesus was received up into glory. How does this
play a vital role in our sanctification?

The Bible describes three transformative effects of the
ascension of Christ. First, what happened to Jesus happens to
us. He ascended to glory, and we too are glorified (2 Corinthians
3:18; Romans 8:29-30). Second, Christ's ascension prompted

the Comforter to enter the world and indwell us. Third, from His throne in heaven, Jesus Christ intercedes for us as our Sovereign Lord, ruling and pleading on our behalf.

The mystery of godliness gives a straightforward summary of the gospel. It points us back to Jesus. Even so, this Christmas season should be filled with loving, longing looks to our Lord and Savior. When our gaze is fixed on Christ, we join the triumph of the skies.

# Reason #17:  Because He Has a Scandalous Lineage

> He is despised and rejected of men; a man of
> sorrows, and acquainted with grief: and we hid
> as it were our faces from him; he was despised,
> and we esteemed him not. (Isaiah 53:3)

O ur Christmas carols sometimes allude to the "lowly birth" of Jesus. Perhaps we could understand how lowly it was if we didn't romanticize Christmas so much.

Jesus was born in a stable in Bethlehem "because there was no room for them in the inn." Shepherds visited Him on that same night. Though we might think sentimentally of these things, we recognize the marks of lowliness in such a setting. Jesus wasn't cradled in a royal crib or a king's palace but in a feed trough for animals. Rabbis and priests and the religious leaders of Israel didn't visit. They lacked the time or the motivation. The shepherds were considered lowclass, untrustworthy, ceremonially unclean. And Bethlehem? That was like being born in Dixon, Illinois. Nothing about the birth of Jesus recommends Him to people who put stock in things like a proper birthplace.

His parents added nothing to His reputation. His mother was Mary. Rumors swirled about Mary throughout the life of Christ, and one day, when Jesus humiliated the religious leaders yet again, they sneered, "We be not born of fornication." The people "in the know" believed Mary had been a little loose, had gotten herself pregnant, and Jesus was the baby. And as for Joseph, he was a Galilean carpenter from Nazareth. Not that carpenter was a scandalous trade. Just that it wasn't an admired one. And being from Nazareth was like growing up in a trailer park in Ozark, Alabama.

But the real damage to His reputation comes from His lineage, outlined in the first chapter of Matthew's gospel. Joseph was in the kingly line of David. But David's line was nearly forgotten by the time of Joseph. If you look closely at Christ's genealogy, you will find more than a few scandals.

The third verse of Matthew's first chapter says very simply, "And Judas begat Phares and Zara of Thamar." Tamar was Judas' daughter-in-law. She conceived twin sons, Phares and Zarah, by her father-in-law when Judah mistook Tamar for a prostitute and hired her. How's that for scandal?

Zarah was heir of the house of Judah until his grandson Achan stole gold and garments from Jericho. After God destroyed the house of Zarah, the inheritance passed to the grandson of Phares through another prostitute – Rahab. At Jericho, God destroyed Zarah's household and saved the household of a harlot. How's that for a family tree?

The fifth verse of Matthew 1 tells us, "Salmon begat Booz of Rachab…." Salmon and Rahab had a son whose name was Boaz. The fifth verse continues: "And Booz begat Obed of Ruth."

Ruth was a Moabitess, a family line that traced its roots to Lot's incestuous relationship with his daughters. Nor does that end the deep scandal in Christ's family tree. Matthew 1:5-6 tells us, "And Obed begat Jesse; And Jesse begat David the king; and David the king begat Solomon of her that had been the wife of Urias." Solomon's mother betrayed her husband and had an adulterous affair with Ruth's great-grandson – David and

Bathsheba. So, Matthew includes four women in the lineage of Jesus – Tamar, Rahab, Ruth, and Bathsheba – most of whom are disgraced, all of whom are tainted. How's that for virtue?

But why? Why would Jesus enter the world through a has-been family with a bad reputation? What was the point of adding these degrading scandals? Consider: The story would change if the scene of Christ's birth included giant fireplaces and heavy draperies and purple and satin and lady's maids and royal decrees. The setting tells us more than what Christ came to do; it tells us what Christ came to be. We learn what He came to do in light of what He came to be. The setting highlights the poverty into which He was born. He made Himself of no reputation (Philippians 2:7).

> For ye know the grace of our Lord Jesus Christ, that, though he was rich, yet for your sakes he became poor, that ye through his poverty might be rich. (2 Corinthians 8:9)

By setting the stage this way, we learn that Jesus came to identify with us in every way – not in our best moments, but in our worst; not in our finest circumstances, but in our poorest. Are you poor? Jesus made Himself poor. Do you suffer? Jesus suffered far beyond anything we might suffer. Do you carry a load of guilt and shame? Jesus carried the sins of the whole world. He did not come to be served, or He would have been born in a palace. He came to serve, so He was born in a stable. He did not need luxury or comfortable living. "The foxes have holes, and the birds of the air have nests; but the Son of man hath not where to lay his head." He was not ashamed of His poverty. He left heaven's riches to save men. What earthly wealth could ever compare to the riches He already possessed?

So, what is the point? Jesus came into the world to save sinners. He didn't come to call righteous people to more religion; He came to call sinners to repentance. He became one of us so He could save us. Politicians sometimes get the novel idea to run for office, posing as a common man instead of a politician on the take. Jesus didn't pretend to be one of us. He was one of us. He was born into a family with a past. He did more than identify with sinners. He became sin for us who knew no sin. And He did this to lift us out of our hopeless condition, make us new, and raise us to eternal life. "That ye through His poverty might be rich."

This is the triumph of the skies!

> And he was numbered with the transgressors; and he bare the sin of many, and made intercession for the transgressors. (Isaiah 53:12c)

# Reason #18:  Because Joseph Didn't Put Mary Away

> Even so faith, if it hath not works, is dead, being alone. Yea, a man may say, Thou hast faith, and I have works: shew me thy faith without thy works, and I will shew thee my faith by my works. (James 2:17-18)

**M**y family and I were visiting a live nativity one year for Christmas. While we awaited our chance to travel the reenacted road to Bethlehem, the host church played a movie about the life of Christ. When the film arrived at that part of the story where Joseph learned of Mary's pregnancy, the movie showed Joseph joining a mob intent on stoning Mary for her fornication. As I recall, the film had Joseph throwing the first stone.

I can appreciate creative license in movies; typically, the Bible does not elaborate on its narratives. However, the idea of Joseph preparing to stone Mary abuses the record. Rather than respecting the story, the film's producer demonstrated his own low view of the story.

The Bible tells us that "Joseph her husband, being a just man, and **not willing to make her a publick example**, was minded to put her away privily" (Matthew 1:19). Clearly, the film's producers did not do their homework on Jewish cultural life in the time of Mary and Joseph. The Bible intentionally sets the integrity of Joseph against the feckless hypocrisy of the Jewish religious authorities.

When these "whited sepulchers full of dead men's bones" dragged before Jesus a woman who had been caught in the very act of adultery, we learn much about their hypocrisy. Apparently, they caught a woman committing adultery all by herself, with not a man in sight. And when challenged to "let him that is without sin throw the first stone," they slinked off one by one, without raising so much as a pebble against the woman. It isn't a stretch to assume rampant sexual immorality among the religious authorities of Israel.

Scripture presents a just man, Joseph, as a welcome contrast to the religious frauds who plagued Israel at that time. And God highlights the justice of Joseph in this. His unwillingness to make Mary a public example demonstrates how just he was. He believed she had committed fornication; the Bible calls it justice for him to put her away privily.

Some might quibble with this: didn't Old Testament law call for stoning in such a case? Not necessarily. Old Testament law called for stoning in cases of *adultery*, though this was not widely practiced.[15] In cases of fornication, the woman's father had the authority to say whether she would marry the man or not. So, fornication did not require the death penalty in Israel. However, Joseph had the power to make a public example of Mary. And God says that Joseph demonstrated justice and integrity because he protected Mary from that disgrace.

At the same time, Joseph showed integrity by refusing to overlook her "indiscretion" or give her sin a pass. He intended to put her away "privily," but make no mistake, he intended to put her away. It was a righteous intention on his part; righteous in every way.

To prevent Joseph from following through, an angel appeared to him. God didn't send the angel with a rebuke for his judgmental attitude. Instead, the angel greeted Joseph with respect, addressing him as "Joseph, thou son of David." Joseph took his rightful place with the righteous seed of his forefather David, the man after God's own heart. And through the angel, God encouraged Joseph and gave him a shocking piece of news:

> Joseph, thou son of David, fear not to take unto thee Mary thy wife: for that which is conceived in her is of the Holy Ghost. (Matthew 1:20)

The angel commanded Joseph to name the baby "Jesus."

> And she shall bring forth a son, and thou shalt call his name JESUS: for he shall save his people from their sins. (Matthew 1:21)

And God meant all this to fulfill the word of Isaiah the prophet.

> Therefore the Lord himself shall give you a sign; Behold, a virgin shall conceive, and bear a son, and shall call his name Immanuel. (Isaiah 7:14)

In simple faith, Joseph obeyed the word of the angel. He proved his faith by his works.

> Then Joseph being raised from sleep did as the angel of the Lord had bidden him, and took unto him his wife: And knew her not till she had

brought forth her firstborn son: and he called
his name JESUS. (Matthew 1:24-25)

Joseph endured the slings and arrows of slander and false
accusation against his wife. He bore up under the scandal and
shame of the charge that his wife conceived a child out of fornication. He must have known how this scandal would play out
in that little village of Nazareth, where every wag and village
gossip would whisper about this "illegitimate" son.

It must not have been easy for Joseph. After all, his
betrothed wife was with child, and he knew he was not the
father. Moreover, it wouldn't be simple to believe that what she
had conceived was of the Holy Ghost. Yet, Joseph laid aside his
suspicions and doubts and took Mary as his wife.

Joseph played a vital role in the story of our Savior's birth.
A man willingly obeyed God towards his wife, believed God's
account of her pregnancy, and followed God's instructions
towards her and her child. This should give pause to every
believer. Follow in Joseph's footsteps, for this is the triumph of
the skies – a complete yielding to every claim and every instruction that God gives to us as His particular people. "Obedience
is the very best way to show that you believe!"

# Reason #19: Because Jesus Beats Santa

He that believeth on the Son hath everlasting
life: and he that believeth not the Son shall not
see life; but the wrath of God abideth on him.
(John 3:36)

W hen I was a boy, my dad preached a message he called
"Satan's Claws." Immediately after that sermon, a great
purging took place in our home. For a few years, Santa Claus
was canceled in the Mallinak home. No Santa hats, no Rudolph,
no "Here Comes Santa Claus," no Bing Crosby.

Now, every culture has its legendary figures, loosely con-
nected to some historical character. What Robin Hood is to
medieval England and the Lone Ranger is to the Wild West,
Santa Claus is to Christmas. Believe it or not, these legends
serve a purpose: they both reflect and reinforce our values.
What is it then about our modern-day Coca-Cola-drinking
Santa that captures the spirit of American culture in rebellion
against God?

Three New York City friends – John Pintard, Washington
Irving, and Clarence Clarke Moore – shaped the legend of our
modern American Santa. In 1810, Pintard paid to publish a
broadside in New York papers depicting St. Nicholas, not as a
"right jolly old elf," but as a somewhat fierce bishop, complete
with halo and scepter. Pintard's print featured a giggling girl,
apron full of presents, alongside a sobbing boy who had no gifts.

Beneath the picture, a poem promises Saint Nicholas, "If you will now me something give, I'll serve you ever while I live."[16]

Washington Irving took up the tale in his Sketch Book, portraying "the good St. Nicholas riding over the tops of the trees, in that self-same wagon wherein he brings his yearly presents to children...."[17] And Clement Moore described Santa Claus as "chubby and plump, a right jolly old elf," driving a "miniature sleigh, and eight tiny reindeer."[18]

Each new version of Santa brought a subtle shift that reflected America's changing cultural values in the early 1800s. Pintard pictured Santa as a judge who came to reward the good and punish the evil.

> To be sure, this kind of Christmas ritual was designed largely for children, while Judgment Day was for adults. Christmas took place once a year, Judgment Day once an eternity. The "judge" at Christmas was St. Nicholas; on Judgment Day it was God Himself. And both the rewards and the punishments meted out on Christmas – a cookie on the one hand, or a birch rod on the other – were far less weighty than those of eternal joy or eternal damnation. But the parallel was always there, and always meant to be there. Christmas was a child's version of Judgment Day, and its ambiguous prospects of reward or punishment (like those of Judgment Day itself) were a means of regulating children's behavior – and preparing them for the greater judgment that was to come.[19]

A decade later, Clement Moore eliminated the elements of judgment and popularized the notion of Santa as a generous benefactor who shows up at Christmas with gifts and leaves us alone for the rest of the year. Moore's Santa fit better with the god America embraced then because, at this same time in the early 1800s, America abandoned the Trinity in favor of a Unitarian God. Santa symbolized Deism's clock-maker god.

We can debate the value of Santa as an object lesson. But the God of the Bible is no "celestial Santa Claus."

> Behold therefore the goodness and severity of God: on them which fell, severity; but toward thee, goodness, if thou continue in his goodness: otherwise thou also shalt be cut off. (Romans 11:22)

The God who reveals Himself in the face of Jesus Christ (2 Corinthians 4:6) is no Santa Claus. The holiness of God is a two-sided coin – goodness and severity. Pop Christianity has rejected this God for a pudgy little teddy bear God with a twinkle in His eye and gifts in His hand.

This idea of an indulgent, doting Santa God has contributed heavily to our modern rejection of the concept of sin. If God isn't bothered by our sin, then nobody else should be either. And if there is no sin, we don't really *need* God. He might be nice to have around the holidays, especially Christmas. But by and large, we have found God very *dispensable*.

But that raises another problem. We can't grasp the goodness of God unless there is severity, unless there is wrath. Why do I need the atonement if my sin is no problem? And if I don't need the atonement, Jesus is just an extra. Convenient at Christmas time, but inconvenient if men have to deal with Him all year around.

The man on the street views it this way. Absent severity, no one needs God's goodness. As J. I. Packer points out, this explains modern America's objection to the presence of evil in our world.

> It is not possible to see the good-will of a heavenly Santa Claus in heartbreaking and destructive things like cruelty, or marital infidelity, or death on the road, or lung cancer.[20]

And this has given rise to the angry atheist, who is both very certain that God isn't there and also very angry at Him for not being there.

> Thus he is left with a kind God who means well, but cannot always insulate His children from trouble and grief. When trouble comes, therefore, there is nothing to do but grin and bear it. In this way, by an ironic paradox, faith in a God who is all goodness and no severity tends to confirm men in a fatalistic and pessimistic attitude to life.[21]

And that is why Jesus beats Santa Claus. Because in Jesus, we see both the goodness and severity of God: severity because Jesus entered our world of pain and absorbed God's wrath against sin as our substitute. Goodness because, having satisfied God's justice, Jesus provides something better than "little toy dolls and little toy drums, rooty-toot-toot and rummy-tum-tum." Jesus reconciles us to God. Jesus gives eternal life.

This, my friend, is the triumph of the skies, and you are warmly invited to join it!

# Reason #20: Because "Out of Egypt Have I Called My Son"

> When he arose, he took the young child and his
> mother by night, and departed into Egypt: And
> was there until the death of Herod: that it might
> be fulfilled which was spoken of the Lord by the
> prophet, saying, Out of Egypt have I called my
> son. (Matthew 2:14-15)

S ojourns in Egypt are a common feature of Israel's history. The patriarchs often resorted to Egypt in a crisis, sometimes at God's direction, other times by their own choosing. In these sojourns, God taught Israel that Egypt was a house of bondage. Then, God delivered His people, and they returned to the promised land. In these deliverances, God led Israel out of Egypt. Yet all too often, Israel brought a little of Egypt back with them.

The most notable deliverance from Egypt came in the Exodus when Moses rehearsed God's command to Pharaoh: "Let my people go." God directed Moses to use specific language in addressing Pharaoh, language that would matter to the Christmas story.

> And thou shalt say unto Pharaoh, Thus saith
> the LORD, Israel is my son, even my firstborn:
> (Exodus 4:22)

When Israel wandered in the wilderness, the Moabite King Balak hired a rogue prophet to curse Israel with a curse. Despite God's extraordinary effort to keep Balaam from this, the prophet determined to have Balak's money. But when he opened his mouth to curse, a blessing came out. Against his will, Balaam pronounced four blessings on Israel. In the third of those blessings, he said,

> **God brought him forth out of Egypt**; he hath as it were the strength of an unicorn: he shall eat up the nations his enemies, and shall break their bones, and pierce them through with his arrows. (Numbers 24:8)

Many years later, the prophet Hosea rehearsed this historical detail about the nation of Israel.

> When Israel was a child, then I loved him, and called my son out of Egypt. (Hosea 11:1)

And Matthew tells us that God sent His only begotten Son to Egypt so He could escape a murderous King Herod.

> And when they were departed, behold, the angel of the Lord appeareth to Joseph in a dream, saying, Arise, and take the young child and his mother, and flee into Egypt, and be thou there until I bring thee word: for Herod will seek the young child to destroy him. When he arose, he took the young child and his mother by night, and departed into Egypt: And was there until

the death of Herod: **that it might be fulfilled
which was spoken of the Lord by the prophet,
saying, Out of Egypt have I called my son**.
(Matthew 2:13-15)

Our Lord has identified with us in our troubles and dis-
tresses in many ways. God did not spare His Son from moments
of crisis but caused Him to experience all the turmoil that
comes with our humanity. The authorities threatened the life
of Jesus, and this threat forced an emergency escape to Egypt.
By sojourning in Egypt, Jesus left a culture that was indifferent
about His birth to enter a culture that was very hostile to Him
as a person.

Egypt was a land of darkness. Rampant idolatry was the
norm. God exposed His Son to the grossest wickedness by
sending Him to Egypt. But though God sent His Son to Egypt,
He in no way intended for His Son to adopt the practices of the
Egyptians. Quite the opposite. Our Messiah found a safe haven
in Egypt. He was not taken captive in Egypt, nor did He find
Egypt a house of bondage, nor did He bring any of Egypt back
with Him when His Father called Him out of Egypt. Consider
Isaiah's relevant description:

> The burden of Egypt. Behold, the LORD rideth
> upon a swift cloud, and shall come into Egypt:
> and the idols of Egypt shall be moved at his
> presence, and the heart of Egypt shall melt in
> the midst of it. (Isaiah 19:1)

Matthew Henry suggested,

> If we may credit tradition, at their entrance into
> Egypt, happening to go into a temple, all the
> images of their gods were overthrown by an
> invisible power, and fell, like Dagon before the
> ark, according to that prophecy.[22]

Whether that happened or not, we cannot say. We know that our Lord left Egypt and that He brought none of Egypt back with Him. And this is yet more evidence that He is the Lamb of God without spot or blemish. Jesus loves the world but doesn't love to be the world. He doesn't love to be like the world or join the world in its sin and rebellion. He came to save the world, and the world He came to save includes Egyptians as well as His own people.

And this is the triumph of the skies. God the Father called His Son out of Egypt. And God calls all the nations of this world, including Israel and Egypt itself, to leave Egypt and to follow Him. Hallelujah!

# Reason #21: Because the Babe Leaped in Elisabeth's Womb

A mong the extraordinary events surrounding the birth of Christ, we have this:

> And it came to pass, that, when Elisabeth heard the salutation of Mary, the babe leaped in her womb; and Elisabeth was filled with the Holy Ghost: (Luke 1:41)

Babies have done some pretty amazing things in the wombs of their mothers. When my wife was pregnant with our oldest daughter, she commented one night that it felt like the baby was doing a complete somersault. Sure enough, when the doctor looked, she had turned herself completely upside down, putting herself in the worst possible breach condition. With all our kids, we laughed in amazement as we felt them kicking and squirming in the womb.

When Mary greeted her cousin Elisabeth, her unborn baby moved in an unusual way. It was rare enough to warrant a unique description: the babe "leaped" in her womb. Only Luke the physician uses this word in the New Testament, and he uses it only three times – twice for John the Baptist's delighted response to the greeting of Mary. The third use appears in Christ's sermon on the mount, recorded in Luke 6:22-23.

> Blessed are ye, when men shall hate you, and
> when they shall separate you from their com-
> pany, and shall reproach you, and cast out your
> name as evil, for the Son of man's sake. Rejoice
> ye in that day, and *leap for joy*: for, behold, your
> reward is great in heaven: for in the like manner
> did their fathers unto the prophets.

The Bible staggers us with this fact: an unborn baby, per-
haps no larger than a bumblebee, out of sheer delight on hearing
Mary's greeting, leaps for joy. As far-fetched as it sounds, the
Bible requires us to believe.

John the Baptist instructs us in this earliest possible
encounter with Jesus. His reaction highlights the importance
of the Incarnation. It teaches us how to celebrate Christmas.
And it instructs us about the filling of the Holy Spirit.

When the angel Gabriel announced to Zacharias that his wife,
now very old, should conceive and bear a son, the angel also
revealed that this child would be "filled with the Holy Ghost,
even from his mother's womb." John the Baptist's reaction to
Mary confirms this prophecy. When Mary greeted Elisabeth, the
babe leaped (for joy) in his mother's womb.

John's response explains what it means to be filled with the
Holy Spirit. Unfortunately, even professing Christians today
sometimes view the filling of the Holy Spirit as some kind of
sorcery. They associate the filling of the Spirit with power and
success, with signs and wonders and extraordinary achievements.

In the first chapter of his gospel, Luke describes three
people who were filled with the Holy Ghost. John the Baptist
was filled with the Holy Ghost from his mother's womb (Luke
1:15). His mother Elisabeth as well (Luke 1:41) and his father

Zacharias (Luke 1:67). What was the result in all three cases? Not a mighty work done for God, but a mighty rejoicing in Christ the Savior. And this joy was contagious, for Mary, Elisabeth, and the unborn John rejoiced and celebrated.

Not to belabor the point, but Elisabeth and Zacharias both prophesied (that is, proclaimed the good news) on the spot. When he found his voice, John the Baptist also proclaimed the news that the Savior is born.

And so, we learn, yet again, how best to join the triumph of the skies. A multitude of the heavenly host praised God, saying, "Glory to God in the highest, and on earth peace, good will toward men." The shepherds returned, glorifying and praising God for all the things that they had heard and seen, as it was told unto them. When the wise men saw the star, they rejoiced with exceeding great joy. So, as we celebrate the birth of our Savior, we too should rejoice and be filled with joy. And we ought to announce that joy everywhere we can. Sing your Christmas carols in the public square. Let the whole world know: our Savior is born! Hallelujah! What a Savior!

# Reason #22: Because Jesus answers our father-hunger

> And they that are Christ's have crucified the flesh
> with the affections and lusts. (Galatians 5:24)

I f fatherlessness is the hallmark of our time, Christmas is the magnifying glass. In a subtle way, some of our most popular Christmas movies have featured this painful reality. *Miracle on 34th Street, Rudolph,* and in a sneaky way, *Home Alone* come immediately to mind. Father hunger also contributes to the popularity of Hallmark movies and has shaped our cultural view of this holiday season.

Would it surprise you to learn that the birth of Jesus answers this deep longing for a father's love?

> And many of the children of Israel shall he turn
> to the Lord their God. And he shall go before
> him in the spirit and power of Elias, to turn the
> hearts of the fathers to the children, and the dis-
> obedient to the wisdom of the just; to make ready
> a people prepared for the Lord (Luke 1:16-17)

The prophecy speaks of the ministry of John the Baptist, whose message was straightforward:

> Repent ye: for the kingdom of heaven is at hand.
> (Matthew 3:2)

So, this message fulfilled the angel's prophetic description of John's ministry. As the nation repented in preparation for its Messiah, the fathers' hearts would turn to their children and the children's hearts to their fathers. The kingdom of heaven is at hand, and this will be the way of the kingdom.[23]

Interestingly enough, the Old Testament ends with this same prophecy.

> Behold, I will send you Elijah the prophet before the coming of the great and dreadful day of the LORD: And he shall turn the heart of the fathers to the children, and the heart of the children to their fathers, lest I come and smite the earth with a curse. (Malachi 4:5-6)

What does it mean to turn the heart of the children to their fathers? Luke describes this as turning "the disobedient to the wisdom of the just." And what will be the consequences for those who will not repent? Malachi warns, "Lest I come and smite the earth with a curse."

So, John preached repentance, calling disobedient children to the wisdom of the just – that is, to fathers whose hearts had been turned to their children. Our Lord Jesus took up John's message of repentance.

> Now after that John was put in prison, Jesus came into Galilee, preaching the gospel of the kingdom of God, And saying, The time is fulfilled, and the kingdom of God is at hand: repent ye, and believe the gospel. (Mark 1:14-15)

Jesus still preaches this in homes where fathers put Jesus Christ first. Because, when a father puts Jesus first, when he "seeks first the kingdom of God and his righteousness," all these things (like repentant children) are added to him. By seeking Christ first, his heart will be turned to his children in a godly and helpful way.

With this in mind, we should consider all the extra family time we have over Christmas. One of our Christmas songs jokes, "And mom and dad can hardly wait for school to start again." Hopefully, that won't be the case. Yet, too often, our family gatherings become a dreaded event rather than a refreshing time of friendship. Erma Bombeck called it the "family ties that bind and gag."[24] You can watch Hallmark movies until your flannel shirt glows, but no amount of holiday smarm will cure the sin that sparks our family squabbles.

Self has a way of spoiling the best opportunities of our lives. And unfortunately, on those special days when the family comes together, Self tends to be the first guest to arrive and the last to leave. Unless we willfully nail Self to the cross, he will wreak havoc on our families.

Our Lord Jesus Christ came to "destroy him that has the power of death, and to deliver them who through all their lifetime were subject to vanity." Jesus can do for your family what no amount of Christmas lights, falling snow, or egg nog could ever accomplish.

One thing that Jesus teaches us to do, once we have believed on Him, is to crucify the flesh with its affections and lusts. And if Christmas gatherings require any advance preparation, a fresh crucifixion must be in order, preferably between Christmas Eve and Christmas Day. Then, with Self writhing on the cross, the family can come together and give as Christ has given – and so much more than mere presents.

The most important gifts we give at Christmas are not the gifts themselves but the extension of ourselves, our love, and our personal presence in every gift we give. And the best exchanges we make on Christmas day will be the love and companionship we share.

As we find ourselves but a few days away from this favorite holiday, I trust that we will set aside distractions, finish any business that might interfere, and devote our time to our families. Fathers, don't let yourself be distracted by events and activities outside your home. Instead, turn your heart to your children and give yourself to them throughout this season. Children, do not harbor bitterness towards your parents, but give yourself to them in grateful love. Every family member should reserve this time for home and loved ones.

Is there not a triumph in this? God can make functional the dysfunction of our families; He can wipe away the animosities and peevish disputes of the past; He can turn hearts to the ones He created us to love.

May God fill your heart with a holy resolve to join the triumph of the skies!

# Reason #23: Because there went out a decree from Caesar Augustus

L uke connects the story of Christ's birth to the decree of Caesar Augustus.

> And it came to pass in those days, that there went out a decree from Caesar Augustus, that all the world should be taxed. (Luke 2:1)

Luke mentions Caesar's decree for several reasons. He wants us to know that Mary and Joseph did not travel to Bethlehem on a whim. Nor did they aim to fulfill the prophecies concerning the birth of the Messiah. Instead, they went to Bethlehem at Caesar's bidding.

Luke's reference to Caesar provides historical context. Historians tell us that Herod the Great somehow offended the Roman emperor Octavian, who ordered the taxing as a reprisal against Herod. Intending to number the people and later tax them, Octavian required all the people to return to their hometowns.

Because Joseph was of the house and lineage of David, he found himself traveling the entire length of the country with his very pregnant wife, from his hometown of Nazareth in the north to Bethlehem in the south. A family would not normally undertake such a journey on the final days of pregnancy. Joseph and Mary weren't choreographing a prophetic fulfillment. But I don't believe Luke mentions this primarily for history's sake. I think Luke means to remind us of God's sovereign hand in this entire story.

Octavian was probably the greatest of the Caesars. He brought the Roman Empire to its zenith and was the most powerful man on the earth at the time of Christ's birth. And he knew it.

We know him as Caesar Augustus, a name he took for himself when he defeated Marc Antony and became the emperor of Rome. His birth name was Gaius Octavius. His uncle Julius Caesar adopted him as son and heir. After the brutal murder of Julius (now immortalized in Shakespeare's play of the same name), Octavian inherited Caesar's name and estate.

Other men have at various times been the most powerful man on the face of the earth. But Augustus thought of himself as more than just that. "Augustus" means "worthy of reverence and worship." While Julius Caesar was still alive, a coin was struck in Gaul which showed the two-headed god Janus, with Julius on one side and Octavius on the other. The coin had this inscription: "The divine Caesar and the Son of God." An inscription found in Macedonia addressed, "To the Emperor Caesar, God, Son of God, Augustus." An Egyptian inscription called Octavius a marvelous star "shining with the brilliance of the great heavenly Savior." Then, in 17 BC, a strange star appeared in the sky, and Octavius commanded a 12-day Advent celebration, "a ceremonial embrace of Virgil's prophecy: "The turning point of the ages has come!"[25]

Romans worshipped many gods, but none more faithfully than their emperor. And during the reign of Caesar Augustus, emperor worship reached its zenith.

So, by introducing the birth of Christ this way, Luke juxtaposes two kings – Augustus and Jesus. Caesar Augustus sent out a decree, which moved Mary and Joseph to Bethlehem in time for Christ to be born. Luke wants you to know this because he wants you to know that a greater than Caesar has arrived.

By providing this historical detail, Luke reminds us that God controls the most powerful of men. But he also shows us the irony of Caesar's reign. His edict brought Mary and Joseph to Bethlehem, where Jesus was born as the prophets foretold. And the Roman Empire saw the followers of Jesus as such a threat that they became obsessed with tracking down Christians to kill them.

Why would Luke bring Caesar into the picture? Why should we care that his decree sent Mary and Joseph to Bethlehem so that Scripture might be fulfilled? Is it not to remind us that our Lord was also the Lord of Caesar Augustus? Caesar was a tool. Jesus Christ is His Lord.

And this! This is the triumph of the skies!

# Reason #24: Because there Was No Room in the Inn

> And she brought forth her firstborn son, and
> wrapped him in swaddling clothes, and laid
> him in a manger; because there was no room
> for them in the inn. (Luke 2:7)

In this day of luxury, I doubt we could imagine the inconvenience of everyday life in the time of Christ. What we call "hardship" was their normal. Our culture expects running water just about everywhere we go – even camping. "Running water" meant something different to them. Imagine a modern-day "couch potato" drawing and carrying the water for the day. We struggle to navigate life without a straw.

Travel was no luxury in that era. A journey from Nazareth to Jerusalem would be made on foot. For safety against bandits and thieves, people traveled in groups, slept alongside the road, and had to keep a constant watch. No air conditioning, no leather seats, no automatic lights. Definitely, nothing nearly as comfortable as a two-star hotel.

Despite the inconvenience, the men of Nazareth regularly traveled the three-day trip to Jerusalem. Joseph likely made the trip annually, as attendance at the three major feasts was nearly mandatory for a Jewish man. But this particular trip – the trip that brought Mary and Joseph to Bethlehem – had an unusual inconvenience. Not only was Mary great with child, but the roads were choked with people as the entire nation scrambled to enroll for the tax.

The nuisance of travel might overwhelm us today. But the Bible doesn't mention it. Rather, Luke refers to the trip in an off-handed way, telling us the reasons but nothing more.

> And Joseph also went up from Galilee, out of the city of Nazareth, into Judaea, unto the city of David, which is called Bethlehem; (because he was of the house and lineage of David:) (Luke 2:4)

Upon arrival in Bethlehem, Joseph found the inn crammed full. A Middle Eastern khan was nothing like our modern motels. There was no "front desk," no private room with a bathroom and bed. Instead, Bethlehem's inn resembled a fort, with four walls surrounding an open courtyard, and no roof. These " inns " often doubled as a protection for the water supply, so we might find a well at its center.

Inside this mini-fortress may have been a few rooms built against the walls. Most people slept on the ground in the court-yard. We can imagine that space packed with people and animals, vendors selling bread, and people drawing water from the well.[26]

With no room in the inn, weary travelers would have spread a blanket alongside the road and slept. But Joseph had a pregnant wife, "great with child." Probably for this reason, he looked for shelter. The Bible gives the crowded condition of the inn as the reason Mary laid her newborn baby in a manger. The stable, which was most likely a cave set off at a short distance from the khan, could provide shelter and privacy for this young couple.

There, Mary brought forth her firstborn son, wrapped Him in swaddling clothes, and laid Him in a manger.

The Bible doesn't tell us what time of day Christ was born, but most mothers would argue for a night birth. After all, who ever heard of a baby entering the world at a convenient time? Babies prefer to make their entry somewhere between midnight and three in the morning.

But besides motherly intuition, we can argue for a night-time birth based on the circumstances in the story. We know, for instance, that the inn was overcrowded. Certainly then, Mary and Joseph didn't arrive in the morning, when most would have been leaving the Inn. So they must have come late enough that the place was already filled.

Also, the angels announced His birth at night. So we assume they made the announcement right after Christ was born. And though the Bible doesn't make this point directly, we know that Jesus entered the world as a light in a very dark place. So it shouldn't surprise us that the light of the world entered in the darkness of night.

What then do we make of the poverty of Christ's birth? Luke casually observes that "there was no room for them in the inn." The world has never had room for Jesus. Is this an accusation against the world? "There was no room for them in the inn" could symbolize the world's general rejection of God. But we have no grounds for accusation on this point. Nobody broadcasted the news of the Messiah's birth until after He was born. So, the keepers of the khan couldn't have known. More likely, there was no room *anywhere* for *anyone*, at least not in Bethlehem when Jesus was born. And in fact, the use of the stable would have been a mercy for Joseph and Mary. Most travelers probably slept under the stars with no shelter whatsoever. The stable shows that the Father graciously provided for His Son.

This particular circumstance probably doesn't illustrate the world's rejection. Rather, it makes the point that Jesus condescended to men of low estate. Given the royal nature of our Lord Jesus Christ, it would seem most appropriate for Him to be born in a castle and laid in a royal crib. Had He been born into that kind of privilege, He would have sent a clear message that He came to earth for the "haves," the "1%," the rich and powerful. But Jesus was born in a stable and laid in a manger, demonstrating that Jesus came to earth for everyone: not just the top, not just the bottom; neither for the haves or the have-nots. Rather, Jesus came for mankind, regardless of station or status.

If Jesus had been born in a palace, that would have been a significant step down from what He left. What of the riches of this earth could ever compare to the splendor of heaven?

And so, we see once again the triumph of the skies:

> For ye know the grace of our Lord Jesus Christ, that, though he was rich, yet for your sakes he became poor, that ye through his poverty might be rich. (2 Corinthians 8:9)

Jesus was born on earth, and if you will receive Him, He will also be born in you.

> O holy child of Bethlehem, descend to us we pray. Cast out our sin and enter in, be born in us today. We hear the Christmas angels, the great glad tidings tell. O Come to us, abide with us – Our Lord Emmanuel.

# Reason #25: Because He Was Wrapped in Swaddling Clothes

> And so it was, that, while they were there, the days were accomplished that she should be delivered. And she brought forth her firstborn son, and wrapped him in swaddling clothes, and laid him in a manger; because there was no room for them in the inn. (Luke 2:6-7)

Today is Christmas Day! The day of all days! For today, we celebrate the greatest gift, the unspeakable gift of our Savior. God gifted the world when He sent His Son to earth.

> For God so loved the world, that he gave his only begotten Son, that whosoever believeth in him should not perish, but have everlasting life. (John 3:16)

God gave the most extraordinary gift – "unspeakable," as Paul called it. We could never describe the gift God gave us and could never exhaust all its benefits, blessings, and value. Employing this gift, God has given us many, many others. God's present to us is a priceless treasure; we cannot measure its true worth. For the sake of this gift, many people gladly gave up everything dear to them, forsaking all to follow Jesus. They weren't disappointed. The Apostle Paul took stock of all he had treasured before finding Christ: his pedigree, his lineage, his position, his status, the honors he received, and the approval he once held. And then he said,

> But what things were gain to me, those I counted loss for Christ. Yea doubtless, and I count all things but loss for the excellency of the knowledge of Christ Jesus my Lord: for whom I have suffered the loss of all things, and do count them but dung, that I may win Christ, (Philippians 3:7-8)

Every follower of Jesus Christ would echo these words of the Apostle Paul.

Before we give our gifts today, we should pause to consider this gift, the greatest gift of all. Like many of the presents exchanged on this day, Jesus came wrapped. But, He wasn't wrapped in anything fancy. He didn't come wrapped in anything royal. He didn't come wrapped in anything expensive. Instead, baby Jesus was wrapped the way we wrap babies in our day. He was swaddled.

I call it the "burrito." The wonderful nurses in the maternity ward are expert at wrapping up a newborn baby tightly in a blanket. I tried to do it myself for a couple of my kids and failed miserably. But of course, there was no nurse to wrap baby Jesus, and the gospel doesn't say who wrapped Him. We only know that He was wrapped in swaddling clothes.

These swaddling clothes weren't special or significant. Or perhaps I should say that the significance of these swaddling clothes was their insignificance. They were common. Probably every baby born in Israel at this time received the same wrapping. The swaddling was universal, though the quality of blanket might differ. And that is the point. When Jesus entered our world, He didn't demand special privileges or set up a cozy situation for Himself. He didn't arrange for any "flowery beds of ease." Jesus came as one of us. He entered the world as the lowest of us, so He could reach all of us.

The angels announced it as a sign to the shepherds:

> And this shall be a sign unto you; Ye shall find
> the babe wrapped in swaddling clothes, lying in
> a manger. (Luke 2:12)

If nearly every baby was wrapped this way, how could it be a sign that Jesus was wrapped in swaddling clothes? The more helpful sign might have been that He was lying in a manger since that told the shepherds where to look for Him. They wouldn't need to go door-to-door looking for a babe lying in a manger since feed troughs were typically found in stables. The shepherds, accustomed to the care of animals, could deduce that a likely stable for Jesus was the public stable at the Inn. So, I imagine they could quickly locate the newborn babe. And, on finding the stable, identifying which one was the baby didn't require Sherlock Holmes. That part would be pretty straightforward. Maybe that is the point.

The birth of Jesus wasn't elaborate or sophisticated. In nearly every detail, His birth resembled every birth in every place at that time. The shepherds would know that they found the Savior because He looked like any other baby, except for the manger.

Can we learn anything from this? I would like to think so. Jesus hasn't put Himself out of reach for ordinary people. He became one of us – the least of us – because He came for all of us. He put Himself within reach for mankind. One need not have a seminary degree or special training in the Word of God or even know how to read or write to find Jesus. He has given Himself to the world, for the life of the world, and in such a way that you can have Him too.

Many families will set all the gifts under the Christmas tree to be opened on Christmas day. Most of the time, we don't put the presents out of reach or hide them or make it impossible to find them. The point is to give the gift, not to withhold it. Even so, our Lord gave Himself. He gave Himself to the world, and He intends that you should take Him as your special gift. And this is the triumph of the skies: the greatest gift ever given is not put in a display case or locked up in a treasure chest. The greatest gift ever given was set out for all to have. Some gifts might be very fragile and require careful handling. But our Lord Jesus gave His body to be broken so that we could be made whole with the breaking.

Hallelujah! Merry Christmas!

# Reason #26: Because He Was Presented in the Temple

> And when eight days were accomplished for the circumcising of the child, his name was called JESUS, which was so named of the angel before he was conceived in the womb. And when the days of her purification according to the law of Moses were accomplished, they brought him to Jerusalem, to present him to the Lord; (As it is written in the law of the Lord, Every male that openeth the womb shall be called holy to the Lord;) And to offer a sacrifice according to that which is said in the law of the Lord, A pair of turtledoves, or two young pigeons. (Luke 2:21-24)

Old Testament law required three ceremonies after the birth of Jesus – one for Jesus, one for His parents, and one for His mother. On the eighth day after He was born, Jesus was circumcised. On the forty-first day after His birth, His parents paid five shekels to redeem Him (Leviticus 27:6). For Mary, the forty days leading up to this were spent in purification because a son was born. On the forty-first day, Mary offered a sin offering and a burnt offering – a sin offering because she brought a sinner into the world, a burnt offering to restore her communion with God.

Alfred Edersheim explains that the two turtledoves or two young pigeons were the standard offerings. Only the very wealthy could offer two lambs. The family would deposit the money for the sacrifice in one of the thirteen trumpet-shaped chests located in the Court of Women. The lamb would cost about $2, compared to 16 cents for the turtledoves. A priest opened the chest at a designated time during the day and divided its contents between burnt offerings and sin offerings.[27]

That Mary and Joseph observed these ceremonies tells us that Jesus didn't live by a different set of rules than the rest of the world. God was no "snowplow dad." Jesus kept God's law because He is holy and just and good, just as God's law is. His perfect obedience to the law brings salvation to the world: Jesus became obedient unto death, even the death of the cross.

Three things were accomplished with the circumcision of Jesus. First, circumcision as a symbol dealt with Jesus' entrance into fallen humanity, "putting off the body of the sins of the flesh." Second, circumcision marked His national identity as a child of Abraham, bringing Him into covenant relationship with God. Third, circumcision introduced the babe to the world, formally naming Him Jesus, as the angel instructed both Mary and Joseph. So, the circumcision of Jesus formally brought Him under the law as a man, into covenant with God as a Jew, and introduced Him as the Savior of mankind.

Jesus had no sin nature to put away, no body of sin to destroy. He didn't need to be brought into a covenant relationship with God the Father, as Jesus was never outside of the covenant. Yet, for our sakes, Jesus was circumcised. By being circumcised, *Jesus obligated Himself* to fulfill the whole law (Galatians 5:3), making Himself the pledge of our justification (Romans 4:11) and of our sanctification (Colossians 2:11).

On the forty-first day, Jesus was presented to the Lord and redeemed, though He did not need redemption. These ceremonies were designed for fallen men, conceived in sin, shaped in iniquity. The Passover in Egypt put a death sentence on every firstborn child and granted a pardon to those with blood marks on their doorposts. The symbolism is evident enough to us – but surely the symbolism in the Passover wouldn't apply to Jesus. On the first Passover night, the firstborn received a special grace. Firstborn livestock was sacrificed to the Lord. Firstborn sons were redeemed.

But Jesus was never a sinner, so He was never under any death sentence. Besides, what coin could ever pay the ransom of our Savior? What could Mary and Joseph ever do to dedicate Jesus to God? Yet, God intended that Mary and Joseph should do with His Son what every Israelite did with a firstborn son.

How strange. Mary and Joseph were the ones who needed to be redeemed, Not with

> corruptible things, as silver and gold, from your vain conversation received by tradition from your fathers; But with the precious blood of Christ, as of a lamb without blemish and without spot: (I Peter 1:18)

But for now, God wanted His Son to be redeemed by the five shekels Joseph and Mary paid.

And so, Mary and Joseph presented Jesus to the Lord at the Temple. He "came directly out of the bosom of the Father, and yet He was *presented* to the Father by the very hands of men He came to save."[28] By entering our world the way He did, Jesus *intentionally* surrendered to do all this.

On the forty-first day, Mary was purified. She must present her son to the Lord, but she must also make an offering for herself. And in all of this, we see Jesus fulfilling laws that didn't rightly apply to Him. Why? Because fulfilling the law showed that Jesus was qualified to be our Savior.

> But when the fulness of the time was come, God sent forth his Son, made of a woman, made under the law, **To redeem them that were under the law**, that we might receive the adoption of sons. (Galatians 4:4-5)

The ceremonies Jesus observed in His infancy came from a gracious God to account for our sin nature. Jesus did not bypass or neglect anything God provided sinful men so they could enjoy fellowship with God. Thus, Jesus teaches us that obedience matters. He obeyed laws that did not directly apply to Himself, that addressed sins He did not commit. In a sense, He washed dishes He didn't soil, made beds He didn't sleep in, and cleaned the mess He didn't make. If the Sinless One subjected Himself to the law, we should too.

Christ's obedience gives us great confidence. Jesus came to save the world, not by being above the world but by joining with us in our sinful state, fulfilling all that was required of Him in that state, and then doing what He was sent to do. Truly, He has fulfilled all righteousness on our behalf. His righteousness, imputed to us, is *perfect* righteousness. By His grace, He provides us with everything necessary for life and godliness. Praise the Lord! This is the triumph of the skies.

# Reason #27: Because Simeon Blessed

And, behold, there was a man in Jerusalem, whose name was Simeon; and the same man was just and devout, waiting for the consolation of Israel: and the Holy Ghost was upon him. And it was revealed unto him by the Holy Ghost, that he should not see death, before he had seen the Lord's Christ. And he came by the Spirit into the temple: and when the parents brought in the child Jesus, to do for him after the custom of the law, Then took he him up in his arms, and blessed God, and said, Lord, now lettest thou thy servant depart in peace, according to thy word: For mine eyes have seen thy salvation, Which thou hast prepared before the face of all people; A light to lighten the Gentiles, and the glory of thy people Israel. And Joseph and his mother marvelled at those things which were spoken of him. And Simeon blessed them, and said unto Mary his mother, Behold, this child is set for the fall and rising again of many in Israel; and for a sign which shall be spoken against; (Yea, a sword shall pierce through thy own soul also,) that the thoughts of many hearts may be revealed. (Luke 2:25-35)

D on't forget about Simeon. His appearance in the Christmas story both startles and satisfies. His testimony confirms the witness of the shepherds and the wise men, and it shapes our view of Jesus.

Consider the character of this man Simeon. He must have been quite old, for he said,

> Lord, now lettest thou thy servant depart in peace, according to thy word: For mine eyes have seen thy salvation, (Luke 2:29-30)

Simeon was just and devout: he walked rightly towards men and rightly towards God. He was a man of faith, waiting for Israel's hope and consolation (Isaiah 40:1). He was a godly man. The Holy Ghost "kept being" upon him (according to the verb tense). The Holy Ghost informed him that he would not see death until he had seen the Lord's Christ. The Spirit brought him into the temple on the very day Joseph and Mary brought Jesus for dedication. And Simeon immediately recognized the Messiah. He held the baby in the crook of his arm (Luke uses an exact word here), and he blessed the Lord and Joseph and Mary.

Consider the blessings he pronounced, for they delight us with the Christmas story. First, Simeon blessed the Lord: "Mine eyes have seen my salvation." Though Simeon must support the head of this baby Savior, yet, by faith, he sees the substance, the content of his own salvation in this helpless infant. Simeon makes three points about this salvation: God prepared it before the face of all people (not for Israel alone); this salvation is a light to lighten Gentiles (Isaiah 49:6); and this infant is Israel's glory.

But Simeon's most important blessing comes through a four-fold prophetic word for Joseph and Mary (vv. 34-35). This prophetic word gives us a Christmas blessing, though we might not immediately recognize it. Consider each part of Simeon's blessing.

"This child is set for the fall and rising again of many in Israel." If we reject Jesus, we reject God. If we receive Jesus, we receive God. God takes our response to Christ that way. Acceptance of His Son is non-negotiable. Those who reject Jesus will fall; those who receive Him will rise again.

How can we be blessed in receiving Christ? If you have been planted with Him in the likeness of His death, you have been also in the likeness of His resurrection. Your fall (buried with Christ) led to your resurrection (newness of life). Others are not so blessed. Some people, born into a Christian home and raised under the sound of the gospel, will themselves reject the Lord. Rejecting the Lord this way will bring a different kind of fall – falling from grace, rising up in self. Such a fall will ultimately end in destruction. In the last day, if you rejected Jesus, it won't help that your parents believed in Him.

This child is set "for a sign which shall be spoken against." Simeon uses a word for "miraculous sign," which means Jesus Himself is a miraculous sign from God. His miracles demonstrated that He came from God (John 2:23; 3:2; 20:30-31), but they did not move hard-hearted men to believe in Him. As a sign, Jesus was "spoken against" – denied, rejected, disallowed (I Peter 2:4, 6-7). To this day, His mighty power doesn't keep wicked men from reviling Him. Friedreich Nietzsche regarded Jesus as the curse of the race because he spared the weak.[29] "The world its hate hath shown...."

How does this sign bless us? Because we see it! The sign confirms the mystery of the gospel, for God has revealed it both in the Person and work of our Lord Jesus Christ and in the words of God (2 Corinthians 4:4-6; I John 1:1-3). The gospel story is as vivid and sure as Simeon standing in the Temple, holding the baby Jesus in the crook of his arm. The unbelieving world claims it is just too hard to know the truth. Jesus says otherwise. "And ye shall know the truth (Jesus), and the truth shall make you free."

"(Yea, a sword shall pierce through thy own soul also)." Not many mothers could handle the kind of hatred evil men poured out on Jesus: the lies, the rage, the brutality, the spite, the cruelty, the mocking, the scourging, the bleeding and dying. Besides Jesus, Mary carried the heaviest burden. The disciples forsook Him; Mary did not. Surely the sword pierced Mary's soul.

How does this prophetic word bless us? The tragedy of the cross brings triumph to our lives. We rise from the grave because Jesus went to the grave. And as we rise, we take up our own cross to follow Him. A tragic triumph; a triumphant tragedy. The triumph of the skies.

"The thoughts of many hearts will be revealed." Jesus is the test, forcing men to decide about Him. Good men, the nicest, kindest, most likable of men, have rejected Jesus Christ. Their rejection reveals their true heart. As Matthew Henry said, "The secret corruptions and vicious dispositions of others, that otherwise would never have appeared so bad, will be revealed by their enmity to Christ and their rage against him."[30]

What blessing do we find in this word? Think of Christmas as a giant mirror to reveal what is in the heart. Christmas exposes the envy, bitterness, and self-centeredness often concealed there. And those who love the Lord Jesus Christ confirm this in their approach to Christmas.

We cannot stay neutral about Jesus. Every man, in his life, will encounter Jesus. And when he does, he will either embrace Him like Simeon or stumble on the rock of offense and be shattered.

> The eye is not satisfied with seeing, till it hath seen Christ, and then it is.[31]

# Reason #28:   Because Anna Rejoiced

> And there was one Anna, a prophetess, the
> daughter of Phanuel, of the tribe of Aser: she
> was of a great age, and had lived with an hus-
> band seven years from her virginity; And she
> was a widow of about fourscore and four years,
> which departed not from the temple, but served
> God with fastings and prayers night and day.
> And she coming in that instant gave thanks
> likewise unto the Lord, and spake of him to all
> them that looked for redemption in Jerusalem.
> (Luke 2:36-38)

A s if Simeon's prophetic word wasn't shocking enough,
Joseph and Mary met a pious, elderly woman named
Anna in the Temple. No sooner did Simeon finish his pro-
phetic blessing than God sent a confirming witness to the
truth of Simeon's pronouncement. Anna entered the scene
"in that instant" as Simeon proclaimed the glory of this child.
Her greeting provided valuable confirmation of the truth of
Simeon's word.

To stress the importance of this supporting witness, Luke
takes the time to establish Anna's character. The Bible presents
her as a godly woman, devoted to the Lord. She suffered a ter-
rible tragedy as a young woman when, after only seven years
of marriage, death took her husband before they had any children. She must have belonged to a prominent family in Israel

because, at that time, it was unusual for a person to know their tribe. She was the daughter of Phanuel of the tribe of Asher.

Matthew Henry suggests that Luke mentioned Phanuel to remind us of Peniel (Penuel), the name Jacob gave the place where he wrestled with God.[32] The name means "face of God," and when Jacob called the place Peniel, he said, "For I have seen God face to face, and my life is preserved." Henry thought this should remind us that Anna also saw God face-to-face in the person of Jesus Christ. Anna is the Greek rendering of her Hebrew name Hannah, which means "grace."

From what we can tell in Luke's account, she had devoted her life to the Lord since the death of her husband. She may have been a widow for 84 years, or she might have been 84 years of age at the time Mary and Joseph brought Jesus to the Temple. Either way, she was a constant presence in the Temple for many years. Worshippers at the Temple would have known her well. Luke says she "departed not from the temple, but served God with fastings and prayers night and day." And, to add to her significance, Luke tells us that she was a prophetess – one of about a half-dozen mentioned in the Bible.

So, Anna wasn't a random passerby who saw a baby and had to coochy-coo it. Like Simeon, she must have been "waiting for the consolation of Israel." She would have known "all them that looked for redemption in Jerusalem," and she let them in on the good news after meeting the infant Messiah at the temple.

Luke wants us to know that this pious woman, well-re-spected in the Temple and well-known as a Prophetess, when she heard Simeon's blessing on the babe and His parents, added her voice of praise and thanks to the Lord. Anna thanked God because now, as she neared the end of her life, she had the dis-tinct privilege of seeing the one for whom she had been waiting.

Directed by the Holy Spirit, Simeon identified this baby as the Messiah, "For mine eyes have seen my salvation." Anna sees what Simeon sees; she also has the distinct joy of seeing her salvation. And she responds to this great blessing with appropriate praise and thanksgiving.

What, then, do we make of all this fuss over baby Jesus? Why does God want us to know about these encounters, about the pronounced blessings in the Temple? What can we learn from these extraordinary greetings?

First, through the mouth of these godly, devoted saints, God reminds us that these things were not done in a corner, that God "showed off" His Son, confirming the identity of His Messiah at every turn. God didn't keep it a secret. Therefore, we cannot excuse anyone who claimed ignorance of the identity of Jesus. On the contrary, God powerfully displayed the true identity of Christ at every possible turn so that they are without excuse. And if God doesn't excuse them, He surely will not give us a pass. He has given us His authoritative witness in His God-breathed words, which identifies, beyond a doubt, His Messiah.

Second, Anna's example teaches us a thing or two about persevering in the face of hard trials. The early tragedy that made her a widow, followed by many years of heart-crushing desolation and a great longing for the promised Messiah, shows us what it means to "wait on the Lord." Anna never grew weary of looking for redemption in Jerusalem. She waited for many years. Ultimately, her hopes and fears were met in Jesus Christ – as will ours be.

Dear Christian, *be not weary in well-doing*. God doesn't require us to stay young, but we should commit ourselves to serving Christ in our time. We may be unable to do what we once did. Still, we should do what we can. Age shouldn't spoil our devotion to the Lord. By God's grace, we should aim to age like a block of gourmet cheese rather than a gallon of milk: spoiled, sour, and chunky.

One final word. Now that Christmas is past, may we continue steadfast in our overflowing gratitude for our Savior. Jesus Christ is born! This is an unchanging historical fact. And therefore, our thanksgiving should be a constant activity. "In every thing give thanks, for this is the will of God in Christ Jesus concerning you."

Anna saw her Redeemer for the first time. She was one of a handful of people to see Jesus in His early life. But you and I have the distinct New Testament privilege of seeing the glory of God in the face of Jesus Christ at all times in the pages of Scripture. So shouldn't gratitude be our constant theme?

And our gratitude ought to find expression in our gospel witness. When Anna saw Jesus, she couldn't contain herself. She had to express her praise, and she had to tell others. Anna's example gives us a good rule for the Christian life: praise God and preach the Gospel. This is the triumph of the skies!

# Reason #29:  Because Herod Hunted Him

> For unto us a child is born, unto us a son is given: and the government shall be upon his shoulder: and his name shall be called Wonderful, Counsellor, The mighty God, The everlasting Father, The Prince of Peace. Of the increase of his government and peace there shall be no end, upon the throne of David, and upon his kingdom, to order it, and to establish it with judgment and with justice from henceforth even for ever. The zeal of the LORD of hosts will perform this. (Isaiah 9:6-7)

Until Satan is finally destroyed, our world will have a Herod. And God calls Christians to defy such men. Christmas offers us an appropriate platform to face down the hatred and animosity of our world.

As we celebrate Christmas, don't forget Herod's role in the story. Before we let sentimental feelings distract us from the real meaning of Christmas, we should remember that our little Lord Jesus invaded Herod's world and gave him a bad case of heartburn.

Make no mistake: God wanted Herod to know that a new king was born in Bethlehem. So God chose as fine a group of magicians as could be mustered to deliver the message. He summoned them with a star and left them off in Jerusalem, where they asked a question: "Where is he that is born King of the Jews?" Their question doubled as an announcement, and their announcement had the desired effect, at least from God's perspective. For their question troubled Herod and all of Jerusalem with him.

The wise men asked the sort of question nobody in Jerusalem would dare ask because Herod the Great was the kind of man to take issue with that sort of question. Caesar Augustus once said that it would be safer to be Herod's pig than his son. Herod executed his wife Mariamne and two sons out of his paranoia towards any perceived threat to his kingdom. When he lay dying, he ordered 50 of the most influential men in Jerusalem to be rounded up and held in the Hippodrome with strict orders that they be executed upon his death. If the people didn't mourn his death, he would at least keep them from celebrating.

When the question posed by the wise men reached Herod, Matthew tells us that he was "troubled" (Matthew 2:3), showing Matthew's skill with understatement. Since they knew Herod well, Jerusalem was troubled with him, like a construction crew when OSHA pops by for a visit. Herod gathered all the chief priests and scribes, which was good since the whole motley crew of them needed some troubling. Herod needed to be troubled because he now had a legitimate rival. And to complete the mix, Jesus made it His favorite pastime to trouble the chief priests and scribes.

In case a well-meaning Christian feels a little compassion over all this trouble, remember that Herod faced the most lethal threat to his kingdom at this very moment. Because Jesus came to overthrow tyrants like Herod. As the carol proclaims, "And in his name all oppression shall cease." The birth of this King announced the end of Herod's kind of rule, of Herod's way of being king. And we repeat the announcement every 25th of December.[33]

Maybe Herod explains why the tyrants of this world work so hard to squash Christmas and why so many so-called Christians have joined forces with the anti-Christmas brigade. Nothing screams "defy tyrants" as pointedly as a lit Christmas tree and a manger scene.

When Jesus entered the world, He faced some of the most powerful men in the history of this world. The Christmas story is set in the context of Caesar Augustus and Herod the Great. Jesus came to overthrow the tyrants and giant oppressors of mankind. And this should give us great joy. As the song says, "Joy to the world, the Lord is come, let earth receive her king."

We should expect that the kings of this world, whether paranoid like Herod or idolatrous like Augustus or despotic like Hitler, would all hate the babe of Bethlehem. So, we should not be surprised that Herod "demanded of them (the chief priests and scribes) where Christ should be born."

But in this demand, Herod shamed those chief priests and scribes. They were the experts, and they had a ready answer. But Herod's obsessive interest sets up an odd contrast to their apathetic disinterest. They knew the answer, but they did not care about the child. Herod didn't know the answer, though he cared deeply – and dangerously – about the child. When Herod knew the answer, the Bible tells us that he "enquired of them diligently what time the star appeared." He later used this information to determine what ages to slaughter in Bethlehem. But first, he made a deal with the wise men:

And he sent them to Bethlehem, and said, Go
and search diligently for the young child; and
when ye have found him, bring me word again,
that I may come and worship him also.

And when they didn't keep their word (a righteous prom-
ise-breaking), Herod ordered the slaughter of every child in
Bethlehem, "and in all the coasts thereof, from two years old
and under." Overkill was the order of the day.

But here is the point: our Lord Jesus came into Herod's
world. He entered a dangerous world, and He came as the most
vulnerable of people. Born a baby, born to a poor family who
couldn't afford so much as a safe place to give birth, Jesus
exposed Himself to Herod's hunting. He faced Herod's hatred.
And He overcame.

And Jesus teaches us to do the same thing. Defy tyrants!
And join the triumph of the skies.

# Reason #30: Because the Child Grew

> And the child grew, and waxed strong in spirit,
> filled with wisdom: and the grace of God was
> upon him. (Luke 2:40)

Remember that Jesus became a man. Luke makes this truth abundantly clear. Jesus entered our world the way people always enter the world. Like all the rest of us, He grew from infancy to adulthood. He babbled like any newborn; He cut teeth; He had His diaper changed; He learned to walk; He probably skinned a knee or two. And He grew. He grew in physical stature, from infant to toddler to child to youth to adulthood.

Jesus grew in maturity. He grew in understanding. I can't fully explain how Jesus came to understand His own deity, His own mission, His own purpose in coming to this earth. He wasn't Super-Toddler, a child prodigy, born knowing everything. R. C. Sproul describes Jesus as one of those rare people known as "super-competent." Most people rise to the level of their own incompetence, but the super-competent never find their level of incompetence. They are uniquely gifted to perform at a high level, no matter how high they rise.[34] No doubt, Jesus was super-competent.

Luke 2:40 prefaces an example of this "super-competence" in Christ's visit to the Temple as a 12-year-old (Luke 2:41-50). And Luke concludes the story by saying, "And Jesus increased in wisdom and stature, and in favour with God and man" (Luke

2:52). But even if we can describe the man Christ Jesus as a "super-competent," He still had to learn and grow.

Jesus' growth fills the incarnation with glory. He didn't become something different than what other men are. He did not cater to the ancient myth of the demi-god. He wasn't superman. He wasn't born mature. He became like us. He grew the way we grow, matured the way we mature. He did this so that He might save us (Hebrews 2:14-17). And yet, His growth outdid ours.

Jesus waxed strong in spirit. His spirit was strengthened by the Holy Spirit, which Jesus had without measure (John 3:34). This points out the key difference in how Jesus grew. He had one major advantage that we don't – He was not burdened with a sinful, fallen nature. So, we see in Jesus what man could be if not for sin. Jesus shows us what God wanted for mankind and what our race lost in the Fall. Sin damaged our humanity, but Jesus proves that all is not lost, that there is something to be salvaged, something worth saving, in that humanity.

Because He had no sin, Jesus did not have the weakness of understanding or will so common in children. He waxed stronger and stronger in spirit. He did not suffer the collapses our children do. Through God's Holy Spirit, His humanity was "marked by a vigour never before seen in a child."[35] He reasoned powerfully; His will was mighty, His judgment penetrating, His discernment sophisticated. He was not easily manipulated. He was not given to fits of temper or selfishness, so common in children. He was an extraordinary man – "super-competent." There was no level of incompetence in Him.

Jesus was filled with wisdom. "Foolishness is bound in the heart of a child," as the Book of Proverbs reminds us. Folly prevents young children from maturing the way they should, both mentally, emotionally, and spiritually. Jesus had a massive head start on other children because He was not hobbled by folly. Nobody needed to drive any foolishness out of His heart. Instruction could bear immediate fruit. The result was a capable young man who impressed the doctors of the law at the age of 12. "Every thing he said and did was wisely said, and wisely done, above his years."[36]

The grace of God was upon Jesus. No displeasure needed to be addressed in Him. God's favor rested entirely on Him so that God was "well-pleased" with Him. Every other man entered this world as a natural-born child of wrath (Ephesians 2:3), but Jesus didn't start where we did. Our experience of humanity is very different. Our progression, our sanctification, always requires us to overcome sin so we can learn to walk in fellowship with God. Jesus had no weights to set aside, no sins that easily beset Him. He could soar.

In these four things – growing, waxing strong in spirit, filled with wisdom, God's grace–we learn our Lord Jesus's holy character. And we can be encouraged by these qualities as we ourselves grow in grace and in the knowledge of our Lord and Savior Jesus Christ.

In a spiritual sense, whatever happened to Jesus happens to the believer. He grew, so we will. He grew strong, so we will. Of course, growth doesn't happen all at once, but we can rest in His promise, "That he which hath begun a good work in you will perform it until the day of Jesus Christ."

In some practical ways, we can join the triumph of the skies. We can join a church and submit to its discipline. Through the church, God gives many gifts to His people. He fellowships with His people through His church, giving the church for our personal growth and development, "for the perfecting of the saints." (Ephesians 4:13-16).

God gives parents to help their children learn to overcome sin. Parents, remember that your children are not Jesus. God called you to help your children become like Jesus. Do for your children what God has done for you. Remember their frame. Remember that they are dust. Be patient and persistent.

Children, please remember that there are no shortcuts. You must be born again. You must obey your parents and submit to their authority in your life.

> Remember now thy Creator in the days of thy youth, while the evil days come not, nor the years draw nigh, when thou shalt say, I have no pleasure in them; (Ecclesiastes 12:1)

# Reason #31: Because Jesus Wins

A t Christmastime, we often hear the reminder that Jesus was "born to die." And that is mostly true. Of course, He came to die (John 3:14-16). But He died so that He might live.

> Therefore doth my Father love me, because I lay down my life, **that I might take it again**. (John 10:17)

Jesus died so that He could rise from the dead. And though we could point to several purposes for His resurrection, the one that fits with our theme is His triumph. Jesus rose from the dead so He could trounce Satan, who for thousands of years wielded the power of death against humanity.

> Forasmuch then as the children are partakers of flesh and blood, he also himself likewise took part of the same; that through death he might destroy him that had the power of death, that is, the devil; And deliver them who through fear of death were all their lifetime subject to bondage. (Hebrews 2:14-15)

In the resurrection, God brought an abrupt end to Satan's winning record. Having defeated every man in death, Satan thought he could triumph over the Son of God as well. And that was his fatal mistake. Because when Jesus broke the power of death, Satan not only lost that battle, but he also lost the war. In the resurrection of Jesus Christ, death lost its power over mankind.

We can delight in Christ if we consider the nature of His triumph. Notice how Jesus trounced the devil:

> And you, being dead in your sins and the uncircumcision of your flesh, hath he quickened together with him, having forgiven you all trespasses; Blotting out the handwriting of ordinances that was against us, which was contrary to us, and took it out of the way, nailing it to his cross; And having spoiled principalities and powers, **he made a shew of them openly, triumphing over them in it**. (Colossians 2:13-15)

Jesus masterfully set Satan up for this drubbing. He lured Satan into this fight. Jesus became a man. He entered our world as a baby, born into obscurity and poverty. When Satan looked at Him, he saw a weak, helpless lamb. "Behold the Lamb of God, which taketh away the sin of the world." Isaiah tells us that in His death, "He is brought as a lamb to the slaughter, and as a sheep before her shearers is dumb, so he openeth not his mouth."

No wonder Satan expected to trounce Him. But Jesus only seemed weak. When Satan took on the Lamb, he learned differently. Sure, Jesus died. But even in that, Satan could not claim victory. Though wicked men poured out all their viciousness, hatred, and cruelty on Jesus, no man killed Him (John 10:18). Not even Satan, who had the power of death, could take His life. In the short time Jesus lay in the grave, Satan thought he had triumphed. And then, Jesus Christ arose. At that moment, Satan lost the power of death.

Sure, Satan continues to win small victories. But many people have slipped through his fingers over the years. Many sinners have escaped death and have joined the triumph of the skies.

> Now thanks be unto God, which always causeth us to triumph in Christ, and maketh manifest the savour of his knowledge by us in every place. (2 Corinthians 2:14)

Death loses power over those who trust their eternal soul to the Lord Jesus. Because though Satan wields the threat of death against us and though he can cause us great fear in the face of death, for the Christian, death is a toothless foe. In the death of Jesus, Satan lost the weapon that made death so deadly. Because Jesus stripped Satan of the power to condemn us for our sin. With the condemnation removed, death became a portal, an entrance into eternal life. What made death so dangerous was sin, and Jesus took our sins on Himself, bearing God's wrath so sin could be punished and sinners could be forgiven.

> Whom God hath set forth to be a propitiation through faith in his blood, to declare his righteousness for the remission of sins that are past, through the forbearance of God; To declare, I say, at this time his righteousness: that he might be just, and the justifier of him which believeth in Jesus. (Romans 3:25-26)

Death holds so much promise and hope for those who have been pardoned. The sting of death is removed, and we rise victorious from the grave.

> So when this corruptible shall have put on incorruption, and this mortal shall have put on immortality, then shall be brought to pass the saying that is written, Death is swallowed up in victory. O death, where is thy sting? O grave, where is thy victory? The sting of death is sin; and the strength of sin is the law. But thanks be to God, which giveth us the victory through our Lord Jesus Christ. (I Corinthians 15:54-57)

This, my friend, is the triumph of the skies. And you are warmly encouraged to join that triumph. If you have (won't you right now, if you haven't?), then you are taught to live abundantly, to pour yourself out in service to God, praising Him and proclaiming His goodness and glory and matchless worth. And when you have come to the end, remember that death is not the end. It is the beginning. For death, that mighty tyrant, has been made a servant to usher us into eternity, where mortality is swallowed up of life.

And all God's people said, "Amen and Amen!"

# Bibliography

Bombeck, Erma. 1988. Family - the Ties that Bind... and Gag! Fawcett.

Carson, D. A. 1991. The Gospel According to John. Grand Rapids: Eerdmans.

Edersheim, Alfred. 1896. The Life and Times of Jesus the Messiah. New York: Longmans, Green, and Co.

Henry, Matthew. 1994. Matthew Henry's commentary on the whole Bible: complete and unabridged in one volume. Peabody: Hendrickson.

n.d. "Historic Hudson Valley." hudsonvalley.org. Accessed September 21, 2022. https://hudsonvalley.org/article/how-washington-irving-introduced-americans-to-santa-claus/.

Margino, Megan. 2015. "New York Public Library." nypl.org. December 9. Accessed September 21, 2022. https://www.nypl.org/blog/2015/12/09/santas-new-york-roots.

Mencken, George Jean Nathan and H. L. 1925. "Clinical Notes." The American Mercury, January: 56-59.

Nissenbaum, Stephen. 1996. The Battle for Christmas: A Cultural History of America's Most Cherished Holiday. New York: Vintage Books.

Packer, J. I. 1973. Knowing God. Downers Grove, Illinois: InterVarsity Press.

Piper, John. 2004. Seeing and Savoring Jesus Christ. Wheaton, Illinois: Crossway Books.

Robertson, A. T. 1933. Word Pictures in the New Testament. Nashville, TN: Broadman Press.

Sproul, R. C. 1998 c1985. The Holiness of God. Tyndale Momentum.

Spurgeon, C. H. 1998. Spurgeon's Sermons: Volume 18 (electronic ed.) Logos Library System. Albany, OR: Ages Software.

Walvoord, John F., Roy B. Zuck, and Dallas Theological Seminary. 1983-c1985. The Bible Knowledge Commentary: An Exposition of the Scriptures. Wheaton, IL: Victor Books.

Wilson, Douglas. 2012. Father Hunger: Why God Calls Men to Love and Lead Their Families. Nashville, Tennesee: Thomas Nelson.

—. 2012. God Rest Ye Merry: Why Christmas Is the Foundation for Everything. Moscow, Idaho: Canon Press.

Wuest, Kenneth S. 1997, c1984. Wuest's Word Studies from the Greek New Testament For the English Reader. Grand Rapids: Eerdmans.

# Endnotes

[1]   (Wuest, Wuest's Word Studies from the Greek New Testament For the English Reader 1997, c1984) S. Ga 4:5

[2]   (Mencken 1925)

[3]   (Wilson, God Rest Ye Merry: Why Christmas Is the Foundation for Everything 2012), p. 48

[4]   (Wuest, Wuest's Word Studies from the Greek New Testament For the English Reader 1997, c1984) S. Php. 2:7

[5]   (Carson 1991), p. 205

[6]   (Edersheim 1896), pp. 186–187

[7]   (Wilson, God Rest Ye Merry: Why Christmas Is the Foundation for Everything 2012), p. 42

[8]   (Wilson, God Rest Ye Merry: Why Christmas Is the Foundation for Everything 2012), pp. 37-38

[9]   (Wilson, God Rest Ye Merry: Why Christmas Is the Foundation for Everything 2012), p. 39

[10]   (Wilson, God Rest Ye Merry: Why Christmas Is the Foundation for Everything 2012), pp. 146-147

[11]   (Wilson, God Rest Ye Merry: Why Christmas Is the Foundation for Everything 2012), p. 40

12   (Walvoord, Zuck and Dallas Theological Seminary 1983-c1985), S. 2:206

13   (Spurgeon 1998), Sermon #1087

14   (Spurgeon 1998), Sermon #1087

15   (Carson 1991), p. 335

16   (Margino 2015)

17   (Historic Hudson Valley n.d.)

18   (Margino 2015)

19   (Nissenbaum 1996), p. 74

20   (Packer 1973), p. 145

21   (Packer 1973), p. 145

22   (Henry 1994), p. 1616

23   (Wilson, Father Hunger: Why God Calls Men to Love and Lead Their Families 2012), pp. 20-24

24   (Bombeck 1988)

25   (Wilson, God Rest Ye Merry: Why Christmas Is the Foundation for Everything 2012), p. 127

26   (Edersheim 1896), Vol. 1, p. 184

27   (Edersheim 1896), Vo. 1, p. 194

30   (Henry 1994), p. 1830

31   (Henry 1994), p. 1830

32   (Henry 1994), p. 1830

[33]  (Wilson, God Rest Ye Merry: Why Christmas Is the Foundation for Everything 2012), pp. 64-65

[34]  (Sproul 1998 c1985), pp. 58-61

[35]  (Henry 1994), p. 1831

[36]  (Henry 1994), p. 1831